Lorraine Hansberry

These and other titles are included in The Importance
Of biography series:

THE *IMPORTANCE OF*

Lorraine Hansberry

by
Janet Tripp

Lucent Books, P.O. Box 289011, San Diego, CA 92198-9011

Library of Congress Cataloging-in-Publication Data

Tripp, Janet, 1942–
    The importance of Lorraine Hansberry / by Janet Tripp.
        p.   cm.—(The importance of)
    Includes bibliographical references (p.   ) and index.
    Summary: Examines the life and work of this African
American playwright and social activist who received great
recognition at an early age.
    ISBN 1-56006-081-6 (alk. paper)
    1. Hansberry, Lorraine, 1930–1965—Bibliography—
Juvenile literature. 2. Dramatists, American—20th century—
Biography—Juvenile literature.   [1. Hansberry, Lorraine,
1930–1965. 2. Dramatists, American. 3. Afro-Americans—
Biography. 4. Women—Biography.]   I. Title.   II. Title:
Lorraine Hansberry.   III. Series.
    PS3515.A515Z88   1998
    812'.54
    [B]—DC21   97–10846
                                                      CIP
                                                       AC

Contents

Foreword

THE IMPORTANCE OF biography series deals with individuals who have made a unique contribution to history. The editors of the series have deliberately chosen to cast a wide net and include people from all fields of endeavor. Individuals from politics, music, art, literature, philosophy, science, sports, and religion are all represented. In addition, the editors did not restrict the series to individuals whose accomplishments have helped change the course of history. Of necessity, this criterion would have eliminated many whose contribution was great, though limited. Charles Darwin, for example, was responsible for radically altering the scientific view of the natural history of the world. His achievements continue to impact the study of science today. Others, such as Chief Joseph of the Nez Percé, played a pivotal role in the history of their own people. While Joseph's influence does not extend much beyond the Nez Percé, his nonviolent resistance to white expansion and his continuing role in protecting his tribe and his homeland remain an inspiration to all.

These biographies are more than factual chronicles. Each volume attempts to emphasize an individual's contributions both in his or her own time and for posterity. For example, the voyages of Christopher Columbus opened the way to European colonization of the New World. Unquestionably, his encounter with the New World brought monumental changes to both Europe and the Americas in his day. Today, however, the broader impact of Columbus's voyages is being critically scrutinized. *Christopher Columbus,* as well as every biography in The Importance Of series, includes and evaluates the most recent scholarship available on each subject.

Each author includes a wide variety of primary and secondary source quotations to document and substantiate his or her work. All quotes are footnoted to show readers exactly how and where biographers derive their information, as well as provide stepping stones to further research. These quotations enliven the text by giving readers eyewitness views of the life and times of each individual covered in The Importance Of series.

Finally, each volume is enhanced by photographs, bibliographies, chronologies, and comprehensive indexes. For both the casual reader and the student engaged in research, The Importance Of biographies will be a fascinating adventure into the lives of people who have helped shape humanity's past and present, and who will continue to shape its future.

Important Dates in the Life of Lorraine Hansberry

1930

Lorraine Vivian Hansberry is born in Chicago, Illinois, on May 19.

1938

Hansberrys buy home in white neighborhood; family is evicted in accordance with Illinois state court ruling; Carl Sr. takes his case against segregated housing to the U.S. Supreme Court.

1940

Carl Hansberry Sr. and NAACP lawyers win U.S. Supreme Court decision against restrictive covenants.

1944

Lorraine starts Englewood High School; wins her first writing prize.

1946

Carl Hansberry Sr. dies of cerebral hemorrhage in Mexico in the midst of arrangements to relocate the family.

1948

Lorraine graduates from Englewood; enters University of Wisconsin at Madison.

1950

Leaves school for "education of a different kind"; moves to New York City.

1951

Takes job at *Freedom*, the radical black monthly newspaper published by Paul Robeson.

1952

Represents Paul Robeson at peace conference in Montevideo, Uruguay; has her passport revoked; becomes associate editor at *Freedom*.

1953

Marries Robert Nemiroff; lives in New York City's Greenwich Village.

1956

Success of song "Cindy, Oh, Cindy," written by Nemiroff and Burt D'Lugoff, allows Hansberry to quit jobs and write full time.

1957

Finishes *A Raisin in the Sun;* in a letter to the *Ladder*, signed "L.N.," defines herself as a lesbian.

1959

A Raisin in the Sun opens on Broadway; wins New York Drama Critics Circle Award as best play of the year.

1960

Writes screenplay of *A Raisin in the Sun;* writes *The Drinking Gourd*, a drama on slavery, which is paid for by NBC but never produced on television.

1961

Moves to Croton-on-Hudson, New York; *A Raisin in the Sun* wins award at Cannes Film Festival and is nominated for best screenplay of the year by Screen Writers Guild.

1963

Hospitalized after unexplained fainting and nausea; results of tests suggest cancer.

1964

Is secretly divorced; hospitalized for radiation and chemotherapy; gives "To Be Young, Gifted and Black: speech to winners of United Negro College Fund writing contest; attends opening of *The Sign in Sidney Brustein's Window*.

1965

Dies of cancer on January 12, at thirty-four years of age.

1969

Nemiroff's biographical play, *To Be Young, Gifted and Black*, opens at Cherry Lane Theatre in New York.

1970

Les Blancs, completed by Nemiroff, opens on Broadway.

1972

Les Blancs: The Collected Last Plays of Lorraine Hansberry is published.

A Woman Ahead of Her Time

In 1964 the black playwright Lorraine Hansberry spoke to winners of a writing contest for black high school students. Describing them, she coined the phrase "young, gifted and black." This now familiar description could also apply to Hansberry. At the age of twenty-nine, Lorraine Hansberry had her first play performed onstage: The production, in 1959, of *A Raisin in the Sun* not only ensured her success but was the first play by a black woman ever to appear on Broadway. She was the first African American, the youngest playwright, and only the fifth woman to win the New York Drama Critics Circle Award for the best play of the season. Later, *A Raisin in the Sun* would be made into a movie and a television special, eventually becoming an American theater classic.

Lorraine Hansberry's successful career encouraged other black actors and writers who were facing discrimination on the stage and screen.

A Pioneer

Hansberry was a pioneer for black issues. Before the civil rights movement, Hansberry supported justice for blacks, urging them to take to the streets if necessary to fight racism. She wrote of the beauty and dignity of black people before the phrase "black is beautiful" was first uttered. She vigorously opposed colonialism in Africa before the concept of African liberation had a name. She wrote about sexism in the 1950s, becoming an early explorer of the ground that would be mined by the women's movement of the 1960s and 1970s. She recognized the struggles of all these groups, incorporating them in the all-inclusive world of her drama.

Before *A Raisin in the Sun*, successful black plays in America were lighthearted musicals in which black actors entertained audiences with minstrel-like clowning. Hansberry's realistic drama broke new ground as the cast presented a serious look at contemporary black life. Her characters portrayed black struggles against racism so vividly that audiences understood the injustices and sympathized with the fight for racial equality.

A Raisin in the Sun attracted large audiences of both black and white theatergoers to Broadway. This was also groundbreaking. Before 1959 few blacks went to Broadway plays because the content did not pertain to them. Many felt that modern plays were written for white audiences.

Hansberry's Influence

Hansberry's success influenced and encouraged a generation of black actors and writers. Most of the people interviewed by black director Woodie King Jr. for a documentary on black theater said *A Raisin in the Sun* had affected them deeply. King wrote:

> In all of the cities the play had toured, young actors and actresses had been moved. The power of the play had made us all aware of our uniqueness as blacks and had encouraged us to pursue our dreams. Indeed, the play had confirmed that our dreams were possible.[1]

Today's readers may recognize Hansberry's name and connect her with her

Sidney Poitier (left) and Ruby Dee (right) in a scene from A Raisin in the Sun, *Hansberry's play that realistically depicted the black experience.*

play *A Raisin in the Sun*. They may have even seen the movie, but few know Hansberry as a feminist or a fiery political activist who spoke out for black rights and defended radical action.

In a 1962 letter she declared that no action was too extreme to fight against racism:

> Negroes must concern themselves with every single means of struggle: legal, il-

legal, passive, active, violent and non-violent. That they must harass, debate, petition, give money to court struggles, sit-in, lie-down, strike, boycott, sing hymns, pray on steps—and shoot from their windows when the racists come cruising through their communities.[2]

Her passions for the American civil rights movement and for Africans' struggle to end white rule were fuel that fired her speeches, her activism, and her writing. In 1959, when the native people of Kenya were fighting for their independence from England, still four years away, Hansberry said in a television interview with reporter Mike Wallace that she believed "most of all in humanism."[3] She hated the violence of revolution, but believed that the Kikuyu rebels who were accused of many atrocities were responding to "intolerable conditions" created by the English.

She helped to raise money. She gave speeches and took part in panels while dy-ing from cancer. At her death she was praised by Malcolm X, Alex Haley, James Baldwin, Paul Robeson, and Martin Luther King Jr.

Lorraine lived only six more years after the success of *A Raisin in the Sun*. She completed only one more play and a movie, plus a television script that was deemed too controversial to be aired. At her death from cancer at the age of thirty-four, she left behind piles of unfinished work. Years before the gay liberation movement existed, during a time when a woman could expect major reprisals for such a statement, she had begun to claim her identity as a lesbian. It was not until the 1980s that feminist scholars connected Hansberry's feminist vision with her lesbian identity.

Her work previewed the African-American pursuit of equality that engulfed the nation in the historic changes of the civil rights movement. Her writing foreshadowed feminism and the gay liberation movement. She spearheaded the future.

1 An Insurgent

Lorraine Vivian Hansberry was born on May 19, 1930, in the segregated South Side of Chicago, Illinois. The themes that would dominate her life and her work began with the circumstances of her birth. "I was born black and female,"[4] she said proudly as an adult. Accepting this identity, she rejected the limits placed on her race and gender. She would not be imprisoned by categories others used to define her.

Lorraine was the youngest of Carl and Nannie Hansberry's four children. Carl Jr., Perry, and Mamie were so much older that she felt separate from them, a child of many parents instead of a child with three siblings. She remembers viewing the world as if she were a creature apart from the others, playing alone with her own thoughts and books for company. As an adult looking back on her childhood Lorraine wrote:

> Seven years separated the nearest of my brothers and sisters and myself; I wear, I am sure, the earmarks of that familial station to this day. Little has been written or thought to my knowledge about children who occupy that place: the last born separated by an uncommon length of time from the next youngest. I suspect we are probably a race apart.

The last born is an object toy which comes in years when brothers and sisters who are seven, ten, twelve years older are old enough to appreciate it

Lorraine Hansberry was the youngest child in a family of four. She claimed that she was viewed as a toy by her siblings.

An impoverished all-black school in 1941. During the years of racial segregation in the United States, black children of all economic classes went to the same school.

rather than poke out its eyes. They do not mind diapering you the first two years, but by the time you are five you are a pest that has to be attended to in the washroom, taken to the movies and "sat with" at night. You are not a person—you are a nuisance who is not particular fun any more. Consequently, you swiftly learn to play alone.[5]

Set Apart by Money

At home Lorraine often felt alone because she was the baby. Once she began school she felt separated from her classmates by her family's relative wealth. In the 1930s the laws supporting racial segregation forced blacks to live in certain areas no matter how much money they had. Because of this, financially successful families like the Hansberrys lived next door to families battling poverty.

Lorraine had certain benefits and luxuries, but she felt like an outsider in the ghetto schools. Her nice clothes and fine home did not make her feel better than the others. In fact, it was she who looked up to her classmates. She admired the independence of these streetwise kids who wore door keys around their necks to let themselves into empty homes. She admired these spunky children who were willing to fight for themselves.

Lorraine vividly remembered one incident that drove home this alienation from her classmates, leaving her feeling ashamed and separate. During the depression, when many working-class families, black and white, had very little money for clothing, her mother sent her to kindergarten in a white fur coat. Although the coat was a Christmas gift, it only embarrassed Lorraine. None of her friends wore anything like that to school. Many years later, she began an autobiographical novel, *All the Dark and Beautiful Warriors*, which included a scene that recalled her childhood feelings:

> At the hall mirror [Candace, the fictional character who represented Lorraine] saw herself and the image in the long panel was even more awful than the imagined one: she looked exactly like one of the enormous stupid rabbits in her silly coloring books. She *hated* those rabbits. Several tears, fat and lush, rose at once and spilled down her cheeks and past her tight lips until they dripped directly onto the ermine.

> She hated that her parents were so proud of the fur coat. To them it meant wealth and success, but to her it meant she was different from the others.[6]

Becoming a Rebel

The book To Be Young, Gifted and Black *contains Lorraine Hansberry's recollections of being set apart in the ghetto. Here she writes of her experience of wearing a fur coat to grammar school, which marked the moment she began to think for herself, to question wealth and privilege.*

"I recall being the only child in my class who did not come from the Rooseveltian atmosphere [climate of belief in the expanded-government principles of Democratic president Franklin D. Roosevelt] of the homes of the Thirties. Father ran for Congress as a Republican. He believed in American private enterprise and, among other things which he had done by the time I was old enough to be aware of him, amassed—in the terms of his community—a 'fortune,' (though actually he had done absolutely nothing of the kind: relative to American society . . . Carl A. Hansberry had simply become a reasonably successful businessman of the middle class). But we are all shaped, are we not, by that particular rim of the soup-bowl where we swim, and I have remained throughout the balance of my life a creature formed in a community atmosphere where I was known as—a 'rich' girl.

In any case, my mother sent me to kindergarten in white fur in the middle of the depression; the kids beat me up; and I think it was from that moment I became—a rebel."

Carl Hansberry

Hansberry's isolation was tempered by her loving father, Carl. He was an educated and talented man, respected in the Chicago community for his success in business and well known for his activities with the Republican Party.

To young Lorraine her father seemed almost kingly. As an adult she recalled him as

> A man who always seemed to be doing something brilliant and/or unusual to such an extent that to be doing something brilliant and/or unusual was the way I assumed fathers behaved. He digested the laws of the State of Illinois and put them into little booklets. He invented complicated pumps and railroad devices. He could talk at length on American history and private enterprise (to which he utterly subscribed). And he carried his head in such a way that I was quite certain that there was nothing he was afraid of. Even writing this, how profoundly it shocks my inner senses to realize suddenly that *my father*, like all men, must have known *fear*.[7]

Carl Hansberry had begun his career as an accountant for Binga National Bank, the first black bank in Chicago. After some years he founded a bank of his own, saved his money carefully, and invested in real estate. He bought apartment buildings and employed family members as managers. Then he went into the real estate business, buying and selling homes and buildings to families and commercial enterprises.

He was a fair landlord and an inventive man who enjoyed tinkering with machinery, exploring ways to improve it. He came up with the idea of one-room efficiency apartments, which at that time were called "kitchenettes." The kitchenette apartments he installed in his apartment buildings created affordable, cheap housing during the depression when jobs were scarce and rent money was hard to come by. These investments and inventions added to Carl Hansberry's success and to the comfort of his family.

Similarly, in 1940 his political activities in the Republican Party led to his running for Congress, where he hoped to use politics to end the system of social segregation. In pursuit of this goal, he went door to door, meeting people and raising money for his campaign. Though he lost badly in Chicago, which was heavily Democratic, the exposure added to his reputation as a leader.

Nannie Hansberry

Lorraine's mother, Nannie Perry Hansberry, was as passionate as her husband about the injustices of racism. The daughter of an African Methodist Episcopal minister, the future Mrs. Hansberry graduated from Tennessee State University in the early 1900s, a time when a college education was not considered necessary for females in general and was highly unusual for a black woman.

Nannie, like her husband, was active in local politics, serving on committees and hosting meetings. The Hansberry home was often a gathering place for black leaders in the arts and politics. An educated, hardworking woman, Nannie expected that despite the racism surrounding them, her children would succeed also. She

Lorraine's parents, Nannie and Carl Hansberry, celebrate a wedding anniversary. Politically active, Lorraine's parents believed in fighting racial segregation.

invented them—with color! The only sinful people in the world were dull people. And, above all, there were two things which were never to be betrayed: the family and the race.[8]

One of Hansberry's earliest memories was of sitting with her mother in a darkened movie theater watching newsreel footage of the invasion of Ethiopia by Italian soldiers. Her mother was outraged at the pictures of African fighters with spears defending themselves against a modern, well-equipped European army.

Lorraine's family expected that blacks would eventually prevail in their struggle. They quoted the biblical passage "princes shall come out of Egypt and Ethiopia shall stretch forth her hands to God" to prove that black people wouldn't always be kept down.

Family Stories

Lorraine's parents were equally concerned about the plight of blacks in their own country and often talked about growing up in the South. On steamy summer nights when no one could sleep, the whole family drove to the park. They slept out on blankets under the stars with the scent of freshly cut lemons and melons in the air. Lorraine fell asleep to the stories of her parents' youth. Nannie talked about the hills of Kentucky and Tennessee and about her mother, who was a great beauty, and her father, Lorraine's Grandpa Perry, who had been born, like his wife, into slavery.

In an essay Lorraine wrote for *Playbill* magazine when she was a successful play-

passed on to them important values Lorraine would always remember:

> We were . . . taught certain vague absolutes: that we were better than no one but infinitely superior to everyone; that we were the products of the proudest and most mistreated of the races of man; that there was nothing enormously difficult about life; that one *succeeded* as a matter of course.

> Life was not a struggle—it was something that one *did*. One won an argument because, if facts gave out, one

wright, she recalled the summers of her childhood and her firsthand encounter with the tales of her parents. For the elder Hansberrys, slavery was not a distant event in history books. Their own parents had suffered separation and poverty, had been considered property belonging to a master:

Finding Models for Courage

Hansberry turned her back on the material symbols of success that her parents respected. She chose instead to admire the spirit and bravery of the ghetto children. Candace, the heroine of the unfinished novel All the Dark and Beautiful Warriors, *described Lorraine's own feelings.*

"Ever since her mother had sent her, in the middle of the Depression, to kindergarten swathed as per the latest Shirley Temple [a very famous child actress] film in white ermine and the children of the ghetto had as promptly set upon her with fists and inkwell, she had been antagonistic to the symbols of affluence. In fact, after the affair of the white fur coat, the child had chosen her friends with intense fascination from among her assailants.

Children such as Carmen Smith and her sister, who invariably lived in walk-up flats where it was very bare . . . and one was permitted to eat good-doing bologna sandwiches on white bread . . . while Carmen, in her teensie plaits carefully parted off all over her head, talked to her mother, who lay on a mattress on the floor . . . looking very tired or sick, and who had to tell the girls about the chores that they would have to do when they came home from school because she would be gone to work by then. Children who, above all, had their own door keys: gleaming yellow metal hung proudly . . . on a string around the neck. Throughout her childhood she had tried various props in fiercely jealous emulation: her skate key, stray keys found in the streets, any number of things, but make believe wasn't the same.

Kids like Carmen . . . had authority and they were loud and bucked their eyes and cursed when their games went badly. They were like grown-ups, and she had admired them mightily.

There had been an aspect of their society which demanded utmost respect: they fought. The girls as well as the boys. They fought. If you were not right with them, or sometimes even if you were."

My mother first took us south to visit her Tennessee birthplace one summer when I was seven or eight. I woke up on the back seat of the car while we were still driving through some place called Kentucky, and my mother was pointing out to the beautiful hills and telling my brothers about how her father had run away and hidden from his master in those very hills when he was a little boy. She said that his mother had wandered among the wooded slopes in the moonlight and left food for him in secret places. They were very beautiful hills and I looked out at them for miles and miles after that wondering who and what a "master" might be.

I remember being startled when I first saw my grandmother rocking away on her porch. All my life I had heard that she was a great beauty and no one had ever remarked that they meant a half century before! The woman that I met was as wrinkled as a prune and could hardly hear and barely see and always seemed to be thinking of other times. . . . She died the next summer and that is all that I remember about her, except that she was born in slavery and had memories of it and they didn't sound anything like *Gone with the Wind*.[9]

Her parents told other family stories, also. They spoke of Lorraine's Uncle Lewis. In 1919, before Lorraine was born,

Onlookers view the body of a lynching victim. Lynching was prevalent in the South, and blacks could become victims simply by being in the wrong place at the wrong time.

Lewis Harrison Johnston was a successful physician who set off with his three brothers by train for a hunting trip. They never took their vacation because the train passed through Elaine, Arkansas, during a race riot. There, a white mob pulled the four Johnston brothers from the train and lynched them. They died for no other reason than that they were in the wrong place at the wrong time. During Lorraine's childhood, Dr. Johnston's daughter Louise was often her baby-sitter. For all her parents' success, Lorraine was not shielded from the knowledge of slavery and racism.

Jim Crow

Because both Lorraine's parents felt strongly about working to improve the lot of black people, they were local pioneers in challenging the Jim Crow laws that enforced segregation. Since the days of slavery, the custom had been to keep the races separated. The Jim Crow laws written in the early 1900s legalized this separation and enforced an inferior status for blacks.

Jim Crow laws affected every aspect of life. African Americans were not allowed to live in white neighborhoods. Their children and white children went to separate schools. In the Deep South blacks were not allowed to use public facilities. Bathrooms, public transportation, water fountains, and lunch counters were all segregated by color. Blacks were not allowed to work in government or in large businesses owned by whites. To be successful, they had to start their own businesses. Sometimes, especially in the South where Carl was born, blacks died for crossing these racial barriers, for not acting hum-

Two black men read an advertisement for a rally against lynching in Chicago in 1946. Lynching was illegal, but that did not stop racist, violent whites from practicing it.

ble enough toward white people. Black men were taught from boyhood never to make eye contact with a white woman. Real-life examples reinforced these teachings. As late as 1955, fourteen-year-old Emmett Till was lynched in Mississippi for allegedly whistling at a white woman.

In the 1930s and 1940s, state laws strengthened segregation. Fair housing legislation did not exist. Whites plotted to keep blacks segregated by refusing to sell or rent homes in certain neighborhoods to blacks. These informal agreements, called restrictive covenants, forced the Hansberrys, who could have paid for better housing, to live in the Chicago ghetto.

The schools Lorraine attended in the black neighborhoods were in need of repair and had inferior equipment. Because there were not enough teachers, classes were split into half-day sessions. Black children received only half the education available in the white public schools. Although she was an excellent student, Lorraine felt the impact of this substandard education. As an adult she called her poor schooling one of the scars she carried with her from the ghetto.

> I am [she said] the product of a Jim Crow grade-school system. One result of that fact is that to this day I cannot count properly. . . . I do not add, subtract, or multiply with ease. Our teachers, devoted and indifferent alike, had to sacrifice something to make the system work at all, and in my case it was arithmetic which got put aside most often. Thus, the mind which was able to grasp university-level reading materials in the sixth and seventh grades had not been sufficiently exposed to elementary arithmetic to make even simple change in a grocery store.[10]

The Hansberrys refused to send their children to private schools so that they could obtain an equal education, even though, again, they could afford it. Carl wanted to attack the root of the problem. He wanted to work within the political system to rid the country of Jim Crow laws that legalized segregated schools and housing. He wanted to work for a good education for all black children, not just his own.

Fighting for Equal Housing

As a real estate man, Lorraine's father also felt strongly about segregated housing. He wanted to sell or rent homes to African Americans freely, and he wanted to move his family out of the ghetto.

When Lorraine was eight years old her father decided he would test the Jim Crow laws and the concept of restrictive covenants by buying a home in an area restricted to whites by law. An owner of the building was willing to break the law by selling to the Hansberrys and Carl's buying the house would break the law he wanted to challenge.

Carl included the entire family in long talks about this decision, however, since such a bold act would clearly affect each member's life. Then he bought a house in Hyde Park, a restricted area near the University of Chicago.

When the family moved in, the neighborhood was hostile and unwelcoming. An angry mob hurled a chunk of concrete through the window of their home, barely missing Lorraine. She was spat on, cursed, and beaten on her way to and from school. During this period, her father was gone much of the time. He was at the state courts where he challenged the legality of the restrictive covenants. His lawyers argued that the covenants violated the U.S. Constitution. For eight months, Lorraine's mother, Nannie, stayed in the house with her family, sometimes with a bodyguard and sometimes carrying a loaded gun herself.

Carl lost the case in state court, and the Hansberrys were ordered to leave their home. They moved, but Carl Hansberry appealed the ruling to the U.S. Supreme Court in Washington, D.C. He spent a great deal of his own money, a small fortune to the family, fighting this case with the help of lawyers from the

---

Hansberry v. Lee

The adult Hansberry wrote many letters to editors of newspapers. In an angry letter rejected for publication by the New York Times *and printed for the first time in* To Be Young, Gifted and Black *she recalled her childhood.*

"My father was typical of a generation of Negroes who believed that the 'American way' could successfully be made to work to democratize the United States. Thus, twenty-five years ago, he spent a small personal fortune, his considerable talents, and many years of his life fighting, in association with NAACP attorneys, Chicago's 'restrictive covenants' in one of this nation's ugliest ghettos.

That fight also required that our family occupy the disputed property in a hellishly hostile 'white neighborhood' in which, literally, howling mobs surrounded our house. One of their missiles almost took the life of the then eight-year-old signer of this letter. My memories of this 'correct' way of fighting white supremacy in America include being spat at, cursed and pummeled in the daily trek to and from school. And I also remember my desperate and courageous mother, patrolling our house all night with a loaded German Luger [handgun dating back to the early 1900s], doggedly guarding her . . . children, while my father fought the respectable part of the battle in the Washington court.

The fact that my father and the NAACP 'won' a Supreme Court decision, in a now famous case which bears his name in the lawbooks, is—ironically—the sort of 'progress' our satisfied friends allude to when they presume to deride the more radical means of struggle. The cost, in emotional turmoil, time and money, which led to my father's early death as a permanently embittered exile in a foreign country when he saw that after such sacrificial efforts the Negroes of Chicago were as ghetto-locked as ever, does not seem to figure in their calculations."

National Association for the Advancement of Colored People (NAACP). It was an exhausting and time-consuming struggle. Finally, in 1940 the Supreme Court reversed the state's decision in a case known as *Hansberry* v. *Lee*. Now, people could not legally be kept from buying or renting on the basis of race. Lorraine never forgot her father's, and the rest of her family's, courage and determination to fight racism. It became one of the central ideas of her first play.

Learning About Africa

In the schools and on the streets of Chicago's South Side, Africa and blackness were considered degrading and bad. In an interview with Harold Isaacs, an international journalist and writer, Lorraine described her experiences growing up. In remarks quoted in *The New World of Negro Americans*, she reveals that even as a child she was seeing things differently from those around her.

To call a kid an African was an insult. It was calling him savage, uncivilized, naked, something to laugh at. A naked black savage with a spear and war paint. It was equivalent to ugliness. Everything distasteful and painful was associated with Africa. This came from school, from the movies, and from our own people who accepted this. In common talk, the term was always derogatory—"You are acting like a wild African!" This meant heathen, unchristian. Most children absorbed this and acquired a deep shame of their African past. But I resented what

Hansberry read the poetry of Langston Hughes when she was nine. Hughes's poems about Africa helped Lorraine experience a feeling of racial identity with the people of Africa.

I saw in the movies and I resented the teachers who couldn't give a more positive view.

This too was mainly about our own American Negro past. We were very sensitive to such things as how the slavery issue was discussed, even in grade school. I resented all of it. I was very unique in that I extended this to the African thing too . . . and even when kids said "You look like an African" as a form of insult, this hurt me, it brought me pain. At the movies when one white man was holding off thousands of Africans with a gun, all the kids were with the hero, but I was with the Africans.[11]

Because these prejudices extended into her immediate family, Lorraine developed pride in her Africanness from other sources—for example, from her books. The Hansberry home was full of books: encyclopedias, world classics, and books by black poets.

At nine Lorraine was reading the poetry of Langston Hughes, Countee Cullen, and Warren Cuney, Harlem Renaissance writers with a new pride in their race who wrote admiringly of their African heritage.

Langston Hughes, especially, wrote of Africa's "beautiful mountains, plateaus, beautiful dark people."[12] Lorraine's imagination was set on fire with his marvelous images and his admiration for his historical homeland. She felt a deep connection to the continent and she began to see a new pride in its people.

Lorraine spent hours with her favorite books. She loved to read about Africa and pored over maps of the continent imagining who her ancestors might have been. Might she be Ibo, Mandingo, Hausa,

Yoruba, Ashanti, Zulu, Kikuyu, Masai? Although the names sounded like foreign words to her ears, they could have defined her grandparents' ancestry.

She and her brothers read Carter Woodson, a black historian, and they talked excitedly about Hannibal, the black Carthaginian general who defeated Roman armies before the time of Jesus. When she was ten years old, her heroes were Hannibal and Toussaint L'Ouverture, the Haitian slave who led his people to liberty.

Lorraine's favorite author was Pearl S. Buck, the first American woman to receive a Nobel Prize in literature. Here was a successful woman who wrote, a model for Lorraine's future life. In Buck's many books, women and people of color were strong and heroic. Lorraine was encouraged: It was what she herself wanted, a world where people of all colors were respected, where the women were equal and free as the men.

Pearl S. Buck was Hansberry's favorite author because of her portrayal of strong women and people of color.

Uncle Leo Hansberry

Lorraine had more than the printed words of her books to back up her pride about Africa; she had her Uncle Leo. A frequent visitor to the family's home was William Leo Hansberry, Carl's brother, a professor of African studies at Howard University in Washington, D.C. The greatest pioneer in African history in the United States, William Leo Hansberry was well known in the field and so respected that Nigeria named a university after him.

Friction existed between the Hansberry brothers. Lorraine's father thought that Leo was not a practical man, not aggressive enough in fighting racism and discrimination. Uncle Leo, however, was active in his own way. He educated people in what was true about Africa, its history, and its current politics. He was able to show that negative stereotypes, like those that distressed his young niece, were false.

Lorraine's uncle brought Africa's rich history right to the Hansberrys' dinner table. He called Africa not the "dark continent" but the "continent of light." He talked with Lorraine about Africa's long history, increasing her pride in her people's past. Lorraine found his ideas fascinating. She began to view modern Africa as important in her life not only for its past connections in history, but for what it meant right now.

When Uncle Leo came to visit, he often brought other guests, African students who attended his classes at Howard Uni-

Lorraine's uncle, William Leo Hansberry, was an African studies professor at Howard University in Washington, D.C. His knowledge of African history, and his friendships with African students, brought Africa alive for Lorraine.

versity. The stories of their lives, and their ideas, exchanged in quiet conversation at the dinner table, were an education for the family. The students spoke formally in precise, accented English while Lorraine listened, intrigued, and learned about life in modern-day Africa.

From her family, Lorraine learned she was expected to succeed, to do well, and go to college. As she grew and began to think for herself, she learned to be proud of her African heritage.

Chapter

2 An Education of Many Kinds

When Lorraine entered high school in Chicago she was serious and shy. She often thought about the things she saw, the injustices her family was fighting. And yet, like all young people, she found she differed from her parents. Unlike them she strongly disliked symbols of affluence, like the white fur coat, and unlike many older black people of the time, she admired her African ancestry and the fighting spirit of the poor. This conflict in her life made her feel like an outsider, like a rebel. One biographer, Anne Cheney, wrote that she

> never fully resolved the duality of her life and works—upper-middle-class affluence and black heritage and revolution. . . . She remained an outsider in the white upper middle class because of her blackness; she was an outsider in the black community because of her affluence and education. Fortunately for American drama, she was an outsider in American society.[13]

As a high school student, Hansberry began to spend time alone in her room, writing. She started a lifetime habit of writing letters to public officials, urging them to act, and declaring her feelings on racial issues. She wrote poetry about the world around her, using the poems of Langston Hughes as a model. Most of her early writing was lost, but she later described her teenage poems as "bittersweet" poems of "ecstasy and disappointment, the discovery of tedium . . . poems of winter landscapes and dust-filled skylines, clouds,

This photo of Lorraine Hansberry was taken while she attended Englewood High School, the time when she began to take writing seriously.

elevated trains, being in love . . . and of existence itself."[14]

As a freshman at Englewood High, she received her first honor as a writer, a school award for a short story about football that she wrote to fulfill an English assignment. Although Lorraine did not particularly care for sports, it was fall and everyone was interested in football, especially the boyfriend of her older sister, Mamie. After a conversation with this young man as he waited for Mamie, Lorraine sat at her desk and created a football story so alive and interesting it was chosen for the school prize. That this pudgy, quiet bookworm had won a prize surprised her classmates, but it was only the first of many awards. Lorraine Hansberry loved to write.

Heroes and Mentors

During high school she also attended her first plays. She saw a folk musical she loved called *Dark of the Moon*. It was full of magic and the summoning of supernatural powers. She saw two plays by Shakespeare, *The Tempest* and *Othello*, starring the famous Paul Robeson, who won many awards for his performances.

Paul Robeson, the black actor, singer, and world-known athlete, was to play an important role later in Lorraine's life when she became a staff writer for *Freedom*, Robeson's radical black-oriented newspaper. During her early high school years, however, he was primarily an admired actor and an occasional visitor in her home. Carl Hansberry's political and business connections served to introduce him to many such distinguished black leaders, and the family living room was often full of interesting people discussing black art and politics.

It was in her parents' house that she met W. E. B. Du Bois, the influential civil rights activist who organized the first black protest movement. He was a professor and historian, a Harvard graduate whose writ-

Paul Robeson (center) stars in Shakespeare's Othello. *Hansberry would later work for Robeson's radical newspaper,* Freedom.

Hansberry's Tribute to Du Bois

That Lorraine Hansberry was greatly affected by W. E. B. Du Bois's philosophy and his life of protest comes across in this tribute, written for his memorial service at Carnegie Hall on February 23, 1964. Published in Black Titan: W. E. B. Du Bois, *edited by John Henrik Clarke and others, it is one of the last speeches Lorraine made before her death.*

"I do not remember when I first heard the name Du Bois. For some Negroes it comes into consciousness so early, so persistently that it is like the spirituals or the blues or discussions of oppression; he was a fact of our culture. People spoke of him as they did the church or the nation. He was an institution in our lives, a bulwark of our culture. I believe that his personality and thought have colored generations of Negro intellectuals, far greater, I think than some of those intellectuals know. And, without a doubt, his ideas have influenced a multitude who do not even know his name.

Now he is dead and his legacy is, in my mind, explicit. I think that it is a legacy which insists that American Negroes do not follow their oppressors and the accomplices of their oppressors—anywhere at all. That we look out at the world through our own eyes and have the fibre [guts] not to call enemy friend or friend enemy. I think that it tells us to honor thought and thinking; to keep always as our counsel distinguished scholarship and hold sacred strong and purposeful art; such as beautifully crafted and humanly involved writing.

I think that this legacy bid us pay attention to the *genuine* needs of humankind and not to the frivolities [petty concerns] which are the playthings of its parasites. I believe with all my heart that the teachings of Du Bois teach us to disavow racism of any nature whatsoever wherever it raises its head—including in the ranks of black folk.

And, tonight, in his memory, I mean to say what I mean and mean what I say: I think that certainly Du Bois' legacy teaches us to look toward and work for a socialist organization of society as the next great and dearly won universal condition of mankind."

ings were the first to pay tribute to African ancestry and address the role of blacks in American history. Du Bois was a great friend of her father's. The two men would often disappear for hours into the library, oblivious to the party going on around

Civil rights activist and historian W. E. B. Du Bois was a friend of Lorraine's father. Du Bois was the first historian to emphasize the role of blacks in American history.

them as they discussed politics and the fight for black civil rights.

Later, Lorraine would study black history under Du Bois. What she learned from him would become the basis for much of her work.

In her own home Hansberry also got to meet her hero, the poet Langston Hughes. As an adult, she described him as "not only my mentor but the poet laureate of our people."[15]

It was as a child sitting at the kitchen table that Hansberry learned about socialism, a nineteenth-century European political philosophy, and Marxism, a variation that has been put to the test many times in the twentieth century. Under strict Marxism there is no private ownership: Rather, the workers own the means of production and, in the ideal case, the whole community runs the businesses, does the work, and shares in the profits. Many black Americans felt that socialism could further the cause of freedom and black civil rights in America. Lorraine Hansberry listened to the conversations, thought about these intriguing new ideas, and began to ask her own questions.

A Family Death

In 1946 Carl Hansberry decided he could live no longer with the racial barriers of the United States. Despite the Supreme Court victory, Chicago was as segregated as ever. Because of their color, Lorraine's family continued to suffer the humiliation of being denied service at some white restaurants. When Lorraine was a junior her father bought a house in Mexico, a country he loved for its warm climate and an absence of the American racism that was beginning to discourage him. In Mexico, for the first time in his life, Carl told his family, he felt free.

He began the process of moving his family, but the move was never completed. Instead, on a warm sunny day, Carl Hansberry unexpectedly died of a stroke while in Mexico. He was only fifty-one. Lorraine was not quite sixteen.

The shock was devastating. Carl had set the direction for the whole family, and suddenly that vibrant center was gone. Lorraine was crushed, and she was angry. She felt that her father's years of struggle in the courts had cost him dearly and gained him nothing. She later wrote, "The cost, in emotional turmoil, time and money . . . led to my father's early death as a permanently embittered exile in a foreign country. . . . [H]e saw that after such

Hughes's Poetry as Inspiration

The poems of Langston Hughes shaped Lorraine Hansberry's view of her world more than the work of any other artist. Hughes's poem "Mother to Son" is like a seed that grew into Lorraine's first play, A Raisin in the Sun. *In fact, she had entitled an early draft of the play* The Crystal Stair. *The following poem is found in* Selected Poems of Langston Hughes.

Mother to Son

Well, son, I'll tell you:
Life for me ain't been no crystal stair.
It's had tacks in it,
And splinters,
And boards torn up,
And places with no carpet on the floor—
Bare.
But all the time
I'se been a-climbin' on,
And reachin' landin's,
And turnin' corners,
And sometimes goin' in the dark
Where there ain't been no light.
So, boy, don't you turn back.
Don't you set down on the steps
'Cause you finds it's kinder hard.
Don't you fall now—
For I'se still goin', honey,
I'se still climbin',
And life for me ain't been no crystal stair.

The poetry of Langston Hughes inspired Hansberry to write her first play, A Raisin in the Sun.

sacrificial efforts the Negroes of Chicago were as ghetto-locked as ever."[16]

He died, she said, "of a cerebral hemorrhage, supposedly, but American racism hclpcd kill him."[17]

The next years were difficult for Lorraine. She felt life had cheated her by taking her father. Her anger clouded everything, and she began to question the things in which Carl had had the most faith: America's political system and free enterprise. His death so early in her life would always influence her view of the world.

Lorraine often wrote about men like her father; men frustrated by the racism that kept them from realizing their dreams. In describing the profound effect of the loss of her father on Lorraine, biographer Anne Cheney notes that "In three of Hansberry's five plays . . . deceased fathers exert such an influence over their children that we almost think they are alive."[18] The action of two plays begins soon after the death of the father.

Leaving Chicago

Lorraine finished her last two years at Englewood High School. She did well in art, history, and English, learning to love Shakespeare. She graduated at seventeen, in 1948. After graduation the family assumed that she would follow her sister Mamie and attend predominantly black Howard University, where their Uncle Leo taught. Once again, Lorraine's ideas differed from those of her family. She wanted to enroll at the integrated University of Wisconsin at Madison, which had a strong journalism department. She wanted to study both art and journalism, and she could do this at Madison.

Even though Lorraine's grades were good and she wanted to go on to college, it was necessary for her mother to intercede with the high school guidance counselor. In 1948 black students were not expected to go to college, and the counselor was surprised to hear Lorraine's plans. Instead of encouraging the young woman because of her good grades, the counselor predicted that Wisconsin would not admit a black student at that time. In the Hansberry family, however, college was the expected route to success and it was Nannie's intention that her baby daughter succeed. Used to coping with racist attitudes, she helped with the Madison applications, and Lorraine was admitted.

Life at the University of Wisconsin at Madison was exciting, but challenging and difficult. Even though Hansberry had chosen to leave home and attend a mostly white, very large college, once there she felt isolated and overwhelmed. In Chicago she had enjoyed a strong sense of community, despite her personal rejection of many ghetto attitudes. At Madison she was not accepted into the dormitory. This was because she was black, but also because she was entering in February when school was underway and the dormitories were full. Eventually she found housing in an off-campus residence, Langdon Manor, where she was the first black student ever accepted.

She knew no one in this huge, mostly white student body, and episodes of discrimination were particularly painful. Cheney tells of a professor who gave Lorraine a D in set design, even though her work was above average. When she questioned him about the grade, he told her

As a student at the University of Wisconsin, Hansberry could not live in the dorm because of segregation.

that he did not want to encourage a young black woman in a field dominated by whites.

The worst part of college, however, was the drudgery of the required science classes that did not interest her. She wanted to study art and writing. She did not see how physical geography, with a four-hour laboratory "knocking on rocks with a little metal hammer,"[19] was going to help her become a journalist. College was not what she had expected.

Lorraine did enjoy the independence, the new people, and the array of political causes that the Madison campus afforded. She made friends with the women in her house and with other students who shared her politically radical ideas. She enjoyed meeting students from Africa, making friends with them, and learning more about their various countries. In her sophomore year she joined the Young Progressives of America, a college political organization. Their goal in 1948 was to get Henry Wallace, the third-party candidate, elected as president of the United States.

Becoming a Rebel

Lorraine was disillusioned with the entire system when Wallace, running on the Progressive ticket, lost to the Democratic candidate, Harry Truman. It was the last time she followed in her father's footsteps by working within the established political system. Hansberry saw no difference in the Democratic and Republican positions, believing that neither responded to black concerns. She wanted the entire system to change. She would next be active as a socialist, an affiliation that offered more scope for her revolutionary ideals.

At this time in American history the cold war between the United States and the Soviet Union had just begun. It was largely a war of propaganda and accumulation of weapons instead of shooting. Socialism and communism became the enemy in America, and the U.S. government kept records on people who challenged American policies. This included activists urging change through socialism

Lessons in Courage

When Hansberry attended Englewood High School, it was integrated, a fact her senior yearbook proudly emphasized. Nothing was said, however, of the racial tension that existed there. In Hansberry's unpublished first novel, All the Dark and Beautiful Warriors, *Candace recalls a race riot and its impact.*

"Oh, yes, she remembered! She remembered, and would never forget, how, on that day, the well-dressed colored students like herself had stood amusedly around the parapet, staring, simply staring at the mob of several hundred striking whites, trading taunts and insults—but showing not the least inclination to further assert racial pride.

Then had come the veterans—volunteers from Wendell Phillips High School and DuSable, carloads of them, waving baseball bats and shouting slogans of the charge. The word had gone into the ghetto: The ofays (whites) are out on strike and beating up and raping colored girls under the viaduct out South! And the summary, traditional and terse: WE BETTER GO 'CAUSE THEM LITTLE CHICKEN-SHIT NIGGERS OUT THERE AIN'T ABOUT TO FIGHT!

And so they had come, pouring out of the bowels of the ghetto, the children of the unqualified oppressed: the black workingclass in their costumes of pegged pants and conked heads and tight skirts and almost knee-length sweaters and—worst of all—*colored* anklets, held up by rubber bands!

Yes, they had come and they had fought. It had taken the Mayor and the visit of a famous movie star to get everyone's mind back on other things again. He had been terribly handsome and full of speeches on 'tolerance' and had also given a lot of autographs. But she had been unimpressed.

She never could forget one thing: *They had fought back!*"

or communism and blacks demanding civil rights for black Americans.

As chair of the Madison chapter of the Young Progressives, Lorraine wrote a letter to the student newspaper protesting discrimination on campus. It became one of the first entries in the FBI's Hansberry file. Federal investigators would continue to track her when she moved to New York and wrote for Robeson's newspaper *Free-*

dom, which was clearly Marxist in its viewpoint. Her questioning of things as they were and her demands for change were earning her a reputation as a rebel.

The Theater and Sean O'Casey

One part of college that did not disappoint the seventeen-year-old freshman was the theater. For the first time she saw the dramas of August Strindberg and Henrik Ibsen, Scandinavian playwrights who created oppressed yet defiant female characters. Hansberry became intrigued by the theater. "Mine was the same old story," she explained, "sort of hanging around little acting groups, and developing the feeling that the theatre embraces everything I like all at one time. I've always assumed I had something to tell people."[20] She began to think of writing plays herself.

One play that especially influenced her was Sean O'Casey's *Juno and the Paycock*. It tells the story of a poor family and the Irish struggle for freedom from British control in the early twentieth century. In *Juno*, as in all his plays, O'Casey steeps his characters and settings in the history and language of Ireland.

Hansberry's memories of the moving speech of the mother, Juno, was later included in *To Be Young, Gifted and Black:*

> I remember rather clearly that my coming [to see *Juno*] had been an accident. Also that I sat in the orchestra close to the stage: the orchestra of the great modern building which is the main theater plant of the University of Wisconsin. The woman's voice [upon learning that her son had been killed], the howl, the shriek of misery fitted to a wail of poetry that consumed all my senses and all my awareness of human pain, endurance and the futility of it—
>
> "Juno: . . . Take away this murdherin' hate . . . an' give us Thine own eternal love!"
>
> Now Mrs. Madigan [a neighbor in the tenement] reappeared with her compassionate shawl and the wail rose and hummed through the tenement, through Dublin, through Ireland itself and then mingled with seas and became something born of the Irish wail that was all of us. I remember sitting there stunned with a melody that I thought might have been sung in a different meter. The play was *Juno*, the writer Sean O'Casey—but the melody was one that I had known for a very long while.
>
> I was seventeen and I did not think then of *writing* the melody as *I* knew it—in a different key; but I believe it entered my consciousness and stayed there.[21]

One of the elements that so moved Hansberry was O'Casey's use of Irish character and dialect. O'Casey used his personal heritage and the language he had grown up with to express the universal experience of grief and injustice. Lorraine began to see how she could do the same with black experiences of injustice and black speech. O'Casey inspired her as a strong model for her own plays, which would use the flavor and sauciness of black speech.

In an interview later in her life she explained her admiration for Sean O'Casey.

I love Sean O'Casey. This, to me, is the playwright of the twentieth century accepting and using the most obvious instruments of Shakespeare, which is the human personality in its totality. O'Casey never fools you about the Irish, you see . . . the Irish drunkard, the Irish braggart, the Irish liar . . . and the genuine heroism which must naturally emerge when you tell the truth about people. This, to me, is the height of artistic perception and is the most rewarding kind of thing that can happen in drama, because when you believe people so completely—because *everybody* has their drunkards and their braggarts and their cowards, you know—then you also believe them in their moments of heroic assertion: you don't doubt them.[22]

A College Dropout

She loved the theater, her classes in literature, drawing, and fine arts, but overall, Hansberry was disappointed with college. She was impatient to begin the life she envisioned for herself as a journalist, and college did not seem to be moving her in that direction. She sometimes ignored her classroom assignments and continued a personal reading program of books by Du Bois and such contemporary writers as the African revolutionary Jomo Kenyatta.

Leaving Her Beginnings

In journal entries published in To Be Young, Gifted and Black *Hansberry attributes much of who she is to the place of her birth.*

"I shall set down in these pages what shall seem to me to be the truth of my life and essences . . . which are to be found, first of all, on the Southside of Chicago, where I was born. . . . All travelers to my city should ride the elevated trains that race along the back ways of Chicago. The lives you can look into!

I think you could find the tempo of my people on their back porches. The honesty of their living is there in the shabbiness. Scrubbed porches that sag and look their danger. Dirty gray wood steps. And always a line of white and pink clothes scrubbed so well, waving in the dirty wind of the city.

My people are poor. And they are tired. And they are determined to live.

Our Southside is a place apart: each piece of our living is a protest."

Sean O'Casey's use of Irish character and dialect inspired Hansberry to portray African American experience and speech.

After two years in Madison she decided to leave college. As an adult she recalled her frustrations and her decision to leave the safe and sure path of college to strike out on her own:

> I shall never forget when [famous architect] Frank Lloyd Wright came and spoke at the University in the brand new and ever so modernistic Union Building Auditorium. There was a rustle and a stir on campus for days before—and finally there they were, he and his entourage *sweeping* in, it seems to me now, in capes and string ties and long hair.
>
> Later, addressing the packed hall, he attacked almost everything—and, foremost among them, the building he was standing in for its violation of the organic principles of architecture; he attacked babbitry [smug, controlled American middle-class behavior] and the nature of education saying that we put in so many fine plums and get out so many fine prunes. Everyone laughed—the faculty nervously I guess; but the students cheered.
>
> I left the University shortly after to pursue an education of another kind.[23]

Lorraine Hansberry wanted to go to New York City: Harlem, black activism, and a chance to write.

3 New York! New York!

Within weeks of arriving in New York in 1950, Hansberry settled into an apartment with three other women on the Lower East Side and devoted herself to serious writing. She wrote articles for the magazine *Young Progressives of America*. She also became interested in labor issues and the peace movement against the Korean War. Her daily life became her education as she went to political rallies and made friends in Harlem, where she moved in 1951 when she took a job with Paul Robeson's black newspaper *Freedom*.

When Hansberry joined *Freedom*, Paul Robeson was no longer primarily a singer and actor. In 1951 he was a full-time political activist for labor and for black civil rights. He was a central figure in the civil rights movement, which his newspaper helped to shape with articles about racism at home, and the exploitation of Africa.

The change from singer to activist had been sudden and unintentional. During Robeson's musical career he had traveled throughout the world. He spoke thirteen languages, and he sang the music of many cultures and nations. Through his travels he began to see a connection between all oppressed people. He favored freeing African colonies from European rule and supported the new Jewish state of Israel, established in 1948. Upon learning about

the ideals of the Soviet Union's communist government, he believed that the introduction of socialism to America would further black civil rights.

Paul Robeson leads a civil rights parade. Robeson became an activist for both the labor and the civil rights movements in 1951.

Daily Life Is Her Education

In 1951 Hansberry
flew to Mississippi to
protest the execution of
a black man, Willie
McGee, who had been
convicted of rape.
Following the
electrocution, Lorraine
wrote "Lynchsong" in
sorrow for McGee's
widow, Rosalee, and
for all victims of
lynchings. This poem
is quoted in "From
These Roots," an
article Robert
Nemiroff wrote for
Southern Exposure
in 1984.

I can hear Rosalee
See the eyes of Willie McGee
My mother told me about
Lynchings
My mother told me about
The dark nights
And dirt roads
And torch lights
And lynch robes
. . . .

The
Faces of men
Laughing white
Faces of men
Dead in the night

   sorrow night
   and a
   sorrow night

Because of his admiration for the Soviet Union, and his travels to the vast land still ruled by the dictator Joseph Stalin, as well as his opposition to America's involvement in the Korean War, Robeson was censured by the American government in 1950 when he was denied a passport during the cold war and the McCarthy years.

During this time both the United States and the Soviet Union had spy networks, and Congress tried enthusiastically to monitor the situation. For example, the House Un-American Activities Committee (HUAC) believed that the entertainment industry was plotting to overthrow the government.

No such plot existed, but ten writers and directors who refused to cooperate were jailed, and hundreds of other talented people not only lost their jobs because of their political views but were often prevented from working at all in their area of training.

The Senate searched for communists with an additional set of subcommittees. In his book *The Cold War,* historian Michael Kort describes one senator, Joseph McCarthy, who

conducted what amounted to a witch-hunt against people he accused of being Communists. . . . Because he played

During a Senate subcommittee meeting, Senator Joseph McCarthy points to a map of the United States entitled "Communist Party Organization USA." McCarthy's zeal in hunting down Communists led to a great deal of injustice.

such a prominent role in the anti-Communist frenzy between 1950 and 1954, those years are referred to as the McCarthy era. Also, the English language received a new word—McCarthyism—which means slandering of people because of their political views.[24]

Robeson was one of many politically active artists whose reputations and livelihoods were destroyed by the hysteria of the McCarthy years. The State Department felt that Robeson was a Communist threat and denied him a passport from 1950 to 1958. Few in the entertainment industry dared to offer him work or rent him concert space for fear of being investigated as "subversive." Even attending a Robeson concert was an act of courage. FBI agents were there taking pictures and getting people's names. Such intimidation

tactics ruined the great artist financially. He wasn't allowed to sing at home. And without a passport, he could not leave the country to accept invitations to sing abroad. It was while his actions were restricted that he started *Freedom*.

When Lorraine Hansberry became a secretary and writer with *Freedom* she was the youngest person on the staff. At twenty-one, she was full of enthusiasm and ideas about feminism, the arts, and politics. She wrote to her college friend Edythe about her new life:

New York City
July, 1951

Dear Edythe,
. . . Fact is, I have finally stopped going to school and started working. Which means a lot of things. I work for the new Negro paper, *Freedom*, which in its

time in history ought to be *the* journal of Negro liberation . . . in fact, it will be. . . .

I am considerably slimmer than you remember me . . . and I think I smile less, but perhaps with more sincerity when I do. I work five days a week typing (eh?) receptionist and writer, and take home $31.70, which I think must account for the slimness. See only foreign movies, no plays hardly; have learned to love clothes in a new way . . . life in a new way. I think I am a little different. Attend meetings almost every night, sing in a chorus, eat all the foreign foods in New York, usher at rallies, make street corner speeches in Harlem, sometimes make it up to the country on Sundays, go for long walks in Harlem and talk to my people about everything on the streets.[25]

In the five years that Lorraine worked for *Freedom* as writer, as associate editor, and later as contributing writer, she traveled and researched stories that would later become material for her plays. Her assignments took her to Washington, D.C., and all over New York as she wrote about Jim Crow hiring practices, about the accomplishments of black women, social injustice in New York, and the peace movement. She researched and wrote about the African countries of Ghana and Kenya, which were struggling for independence.

The job sharpened her writing skills and strengthened her interest in political activism as she covered events such as the Washington, D.C., conference "Sojourners for Truth." At this meeting, 132 black women demanded that the Department of Justice end violence and lynching in the South. Many of the participants had lost husbands and sons to lynching and beatings. She met a Mrs. Westry, whose son's eyes had been gouged out by police officers, who then shot the young man dead on the operating table.

Speaking Out for Paul Robeson

In March 1952 Hansberry made her most important *Freedom* trip, an event she later spoke of as key in her life. Because Robeson's passport had been revoked, he could not attend the Inter-Continental Peace Conference in Uruguay, where he had been invited to speak. Instead, Lorraine was sent. She was able to pass by officials

Hansberry works on Freedom *newspaper. Through her work at the newspaper, Hansberry was able to represent Robeson at a conference in Uruguay.*

unnoticed and board the plane to Uruguay. Unfortunately, the flight was so bumpy and perilous that it left Lorraine with a fear of flying. She avoided all planes from that time on.

In Montevideo she was honored at a special session for women, where she was presented with flowers. Later, she was given Robeson's place on the stage at the principal ceremonies. Speaking in his name, she urged world peace and protested the Korean War, which both she and Robeson felt was an aggressive act to extend U.S. power and control in Asia, under cover of the cold war. She stood, thrilled, as five thousand people chanted "Viva Robeson." Returning home she learned that now her own passport had been revoked. Undaunted, she wrote a story about her experiences, which was published in *Freedom*.

An Inspiration and a Warning

It was exceptional to find a woman as young as Hansberry being given so much responsibility. The opportunity to speak out and be heard, to represent Robeson and her people, strengthened her as a speaker and as a writer. Standing with thousands of delegates in South America, she recognized that she was not a minority, but part of a world population: people of color, people for peace and freedom.

Biographer Anne Cheney states that because of Robeson, Lorraine "began to consider the fusion of art and politics." She did so, however, with an awareness that commitment can have dangerous consequences. Robeson was, says Cheney, "an inspiration and, to some extent, a warning."[26]

Robeson was the subject of Hansberry's first attempt at playwriting, a script for a variety show fund-raiser held in Harlem as a tribute to Robeson. "Pulse of the Peoples 1954: A Cultural Salute to Paul Robeson" raised enough money to continue to pay attorneys and file appeals to have the State Department's decision reversed and Robeson's passport returned. In the script she praised Robeson as "a truly great artist . . . who embod-

Through appeals courts, Paul Robeson eventually was able to get his passport returned. He never was able to regain his career, however.

ies . . . at once—not only in his life but in his art—the people from whom he springs: to be a voice, member and champion of the people's struggle." [27]

Hansberry wrote to her friend Edythe about her despair at seeing the government's actions in the cold war and the anti-Communist "witch hunts." She called the treatment of Robeson "fascist" because the government was using its power against a citizen to silence his ideas and his voice. She compared living with the threat of such abuses to the recent experiences of the German people under the dictator Adolf Hitler. Opposing ideas were not allowed.

> Certainly I feel closer to what is happening than you perhaps yet feel. I know many who have already been lapped up by this new [Nazi] terror . . . know the arrests in the early morning, the shifty-eyed ones who follow, follow, follow . . . and know the people who are the victims: the quiet and the courageous. Frankly, I would not have thought the caliber of humanity to be so sturdy after such spheres of corruption have surrounded it. But it is so.

> Quite simply and quietly as I know how to say it; I am sick of poverty, lynching, stupid wars and the universal maltreatment of my people and obsessed with a rather desperate desire for a new world for me and my brothers. [28]

Freedom Offices and Alice Childress

The *Freedom* offices were in a loft at 53 West 125th Street in Harlem. The same ad-

Playwright Alice Childress also wrote for Freedom *and became one of Hansberry's friends. Childress's success as a playwright inspired Hansberry.*

dress housed Dr. W. E. B. Du Bois and the Council on African Affairs. It was a busy place, with narrow rooms full of dedicated workers. Eslanda Robeson, Paul's wife, a writer and correspondent for the United Nations, was there. Well-known socialist Shirley Graham Du Bois, wife of W. E. B. Du Bois, wrote for the paper, as did actress and playwright Alice Childress.

Childress became a friend of Lorraine's. They belonged to the same black writing groups: the Committee for the Negro in the Arts and the Harlem Writers Workshop. Both women were writers, and Childress's success (she was the first black

I Was Born Black and Female

In a speech to writers published in the Black Scholar, *an academic journal of black studies and research published in Oakland, California, Hansberry made a connection between racism and sexism.*

"I was born on the South Side of Chicago. I was born black and a female. I was born in a depression after one world war, and came into my adolescence during another. While I was still in my teens the first atom bombs were dropped on human beings at Nagasaki and Hiroshima, and by the time I was twenty-three years old my government and that of the Soviet Union had entered actively into the worst conflict of nerves in human history—the Cold War.

I have lost friends and relatives through cancer, lynching and war. I have been personally the victim of physical attack which was the offspring of racial and political hysteria. . . . I see daily on the streets of New York, street gangs and prostitutes and beggars. I have, like all of you, on a thousand occasions seen indescribable displays of man's very real inhumanity to man; and I have come to maturity, as we all must, knowing that greed and malice and indifference to human misery, bigotry and corruption, brutality and, perhaps above all else, ignorance—the prime ancient and persistent enemy of (hu)man(s)—abound in this world.

I say all of this to say that one cannot live with sighted eyes and feeling heart and not know and react to the miseries which afflict this world.

I have given you this account so that you know that what I write is not based on the assumption of idyllic possibilities or innocent assessments of the true nature of life—but, rather, my own personal view that, posing one against the other, I think the human race does command its own destiny and that that destiny can eventually embrace the stars."

woman to have a play produced off-Broadway) encouraged Hansberry. Childress wrote about poor, forgotten people.

Her main characters were black women who refused to be victims. One such character, Mildred, was a plainspoken, no-

nonsense maid created by Childress for a regular column she wrote for *Freedom*. Mildred was funny, but there was biting truth beneath the humor.

Childress was not only a friend, she was a role model: a successful black female playwright who wrote about courageous, spunky black women. Hansberry's friend Edythe, from Madison, the women on the *Freedom* staff, and women she worked with in the civil rights movement were important to her growth.

Steven Carter, in his book *Hansberry's Drama*, wrote about this source of Lorraine's strength: the model of strong black women.

> Hansberry drew constant inspiration and strength from the courage and resourcefulness of the women she met and saw daily, their ability to "keep on keeping on," and from the historic role of black women in the fight for survival and transcendence of their people. As she noted in an interview with [well-known Chicago journalist and social commentator] Studs Terkel: "Obviously the most oppressed group of any oppressed group will be its women, who are twice oppressed. So I should imagine that they react accordingly: As oppression makes people more militant, women become *twice* militant, because they are twice oppressed."[29]

Louis Burnham, Chief Editor

Without a doubt, the person on the *Freedom* staff who most influenced Lorraine was its editor, Louis Burnham. He was a slight, poetic black man who in the 1930s and 1940s had been a founder and hero of the Southern Negro Youth Congress. Burnham encouraged Lorraine's writing, not only her newspaper reporting, but the plays she was working on and *All the Dark and Beautiful Warriors*, a novel based on her college days, begun at age eighteen. At twenty she was afraid she had changed too much to write about college life, but Burnham encouraged her to continue.

Burnham handpicked assignments for Lorraine that catered to her revolutionary spirit while strengthening her writing skills. He sent Hansberry out to report on social issues in New York. She interviewed blacks who had been wrongly accused of crimes and attorneys who had defended black Communist leaders and then found themselves jailed on charges of contempt of court. She wrote about unfair hiring practices in which black workers were kept from the better-paying jobs, about the inadequacies of Harlem schools, and about juvenile crime.

Lorraine blamed crime committed by juveniles on their poor self-image. They had not been taught pride in themselves and their black and African heritage. Instead of learning about black accomplishments and heroes, Hansberry states, teenagers read negative descriptions of their race. In "Life Challenges Negro Youth," she quotes one such demeaning description of the black people of the Haitian Revolution:

> The failure to grasp subjective ideas, the strong sexual and herd instinct with few inhibitions, the simple dream life, the easy reversion to savagery when deprived of the restraining

influence of the whites, as in Haiti . . . all these and many other things betray the savage heart beneath the civilized exterior.

Hansberry then writes:

The program of historical and cultural obliteration neither begins nor ends

Louis E. Burnham, Editor

An excerpt from Hansberry's papers, found in To Be Young, Gifted and Black, *shows the admiration she held for her* Freedom *editor, Louis E. Burnham.*

"The editor wore a large black moustache in those days and he was seated in an office on Lenox Avenue behind a desk arranged in front of a large curving window that allowed one to see a lot of Harlem at one time. It seems to me now that there were few things in that office other than the desk, the two chairs we sat on, a lonely typewriter, some panels of gray afternoon light—and the altogether commanding personality of Louis E. Burnham.

His voice was very deep and his language struck my senses immediately with its profound literacy, constantly punctuated by deliberate and loving poetic lapses into the beloved color of the speech of the masses of our people. He invariably made his eyes very wide when he said things in idiom [black speech] and, sometimes, in the middle of a story, he just opened his mouth and howled for the joy of it. I suppose it was because of his voice, so rich, so strong, so very certain, that I never associated fragility with Louis Burnham despite his slight frame.

The things he taught me were great things: that all racism was rotten, white or black, that *everything* is political; that people tend to be indescribably beautiful and uproariously funny. He also taught me that they have enemies who are grotesque and that freedom lies in the recognition of all of that and other things. . . .

I recall how he kept turning back and forth from that window that let him look at Harlem while he talked to me. The thing he had for our people was something marvelous; he gave part of it to me and I shall die with it as he did. He would say simply, 'They are beautiful, child,' and close his eyes sometimes. And I always knew that he could see them marching then.

It was an open and adoring love that mawkishness [excessive sentimentality] never touched."

with school experiences. Awaiting our youth in every area of American life is a barrage of propaganda which distorts and disparages their identity.

In a land where the Grace Kelly–Marilyn Monroe monotyped "ideal" is imposed on the national culture, racist logic insists that anything directly opposite—no matter how lovely—is "naturally" ugly.

Being "taught that they are un-beautiful, without culture or history," Hansberry reasons, has had "ravaging effects on generations of American Negroes."[30]

Biographer Margaret B. Wilkerson writes that it was as a young reporter for *Freedom* that Hansberry's revolutionary spirit became "radicalized." Writing for Burnham she grew increasingly "aware of the injustices perpetrated in the name of democracy, and the formidable . . . forces arrayed to maintain an insensitive system of government."[31] Society would not change on its own, however; she and others like her must make the change, must create the justice black people longed for.

Lorraine was not content only to write about the social ills exposed in her research for *Freedom* assignments. She went out into the streets to attend rallies and speeches. She helped move dispossessed black families back into their homes to fight unfair housing regulations. She demonstrated in Times Square against lynching, while watching police on horseback ride down demonstrators.

Study with Du Bois

While Hansberry was writing for *Freedom* she studied African history under W. E. B.

W. E. B. Du Bois did not escape the long arm of McCarthy's anti-Communist campaign and was arrested for his views. Lack of evidence propelled his quick release.

Du Bois at the Jefferson School of Social Science. Du Bois's writings were the first black scholarly analysis of the African ancestry of millions of U.S. citizens and of the role of blacks in American history. The protest movement he started turned into the influential National Association for the Advancement of Colored People (NAACP). Du Bois was a socialist, and his writing strengthened Hansberry's belief that socialism would solve many injustices that made black life in America so difficult.

Lorraine Hansberry's biographer Anne Cheney credits Du Bois with an important role in the playwright's artistic development. "Of his numerous works, *Black Folk: Then and Now* affected her most obviously and specifically. . . . [Du Bois's] moral purpose in writing [this book] was to dispute the notion that the Negro has no history and to shatter the black man's image as 'the clown of history' and 'the slave of industry.' "[32] Many of her plays are rich with information from her studies with Du Bois.

In her library, on the inside flap of her copy of *Black Folk: Then and Now*, Hansberry had written her description of her teacher as she sat in his classroom: "Freedom's passion, organized and refined, sits there."[33] It was with great sadness that a furious Hansberry watched the arrest of eighty-three-year-old Dr. Du Bois during the years of the McCarthy hearings. He was handcuffed and fingerprinted, and put on trial for being a "foreign agent" and a risk to national security. In the end, the charges were dismissed, the judge declaring that the government had no case.

Theater

For entertainment Hansberry continued to attend the theater and began to make friends among the members of small acting groups. Suddenly she recognized that theater offered opportunities to engage in all the things most important to her: writing, protesting, and communicating with her people. She described her realization of the power of theater as a small explosion in her life. Knocking her fist into the palm of her hand, she told an interviewer, "The theatre came into my life like K-pow!"[34]

Hansberry began to think about writing plays herself. She felt theater could be a laboratory to study human experience and that playwriting could be as powerful as letters to the editor and protests on picket lines. She could talk to people through her art as clearly as by marching in the streets—more clearly, in fact, because she could reach more people.

Meeting Bobby

Lorraine remained extremely busy with her work, theater projects, and social activism. She was picketing to protest the exclusion of blacks from the New York University basketball team when she met Robert Nemiroff, her future husband. The son of Russian Jewish parents who owned a small international restaurant in Greenwich Village, Nemiroff was a student of literature at NYU. He shared with Lorraine a commitment to activism and an interest in arts and culture.

Although Nemiroff was white, Lorraine felt his Jewish heritage gave him a deep understanding of the injustice of oppression. Both blacks and Jews had been held captive in foreign lands. Lorraine described the Jews as "The only people [my forebears] had ever heard of who 'got away'—and that proudly—from bondage."[35]

The couple began dating. Although interracial marriage was illegal in thirty states, the atmosphere of New York City in general and Greenwich Village in particular was more accepting. Hansberry's family, however, disliked seeing a white man in love with Lorraine. There had never been an interracial couple in the family, and they were not pleased with this development.

On the other hand, the Hansberrys were calmed by the idea that Lorraine had a man in her life. Her mother wanted her to marry. As sister Mamie described to biographer Anne Cheney:

Mother was bugging her about coming home after she had been in New York a couple of years or so. She said, "Well, any middle-class lady shouldn't be in New York so long, because you know it is time for you to think about getting married, and you know." I think [Lorraine] had two or three roommates, and Mother began to say, "Well, it is time you were getting married, time you started looking for a husband. . . ." Lorraine kept saying, "Yes, well, I am busy and I am happy." "Yes, [mother replied] but you ought to think about getting married, and just girls setting in an apartment isn't safe, and it will subject you to ridicule and all that stuff."[36]

It was not an easy time for Lorraine. She wasn't sure what her main work should be—activism (working for the rights of her people) or writing. Even in her writing she was torn. Should she focus on journalism or playwriting?

Lorraine was enjoying her independence and her active life. Although she loved Nemiroff, she wasn't at all convinced that marriage was right for her. Influenced by the French feminist Simone de Beauvoir, she rejected the idea that marriage and motherhood were the only roles for women. Hansberry came to agree with de Beauvoir that marriage was a social trap women were forced into because of the limits society placed on their lives. Of the French author's book *The Second Sex*, she said simply, "Reading it changed my life."[37]

In an unpublished essay, ironically entitled "In Defense of the Equality of Man," Lorraine wrote:

The glaring fact is that Mom's life needs liberation as much as everyone else's. To say so is to be thought of as

attacking the "bedrock of our way of life," . . . but it must be said. Mom must be allowed to think of herself, as Simone de Beauvoir has insisted brilliantly, as a human being first and a mother second. Housewives insist on identifying themselves . . . as "*only* housewives" because, apparently, they perceive that housework and care of the family is but humankind's necessity of function. . . . We do not live to wash our faces and eat our meals, we wash our faces and eat our meals in order to participate in the world: in the classroom, in the factory, in the office, in the shop, in the national and international halls of government, in the scientific laboratory and in the studios where the arts are created. *The Feminists did not create the housewife's dissatisfaction with her lot—the Feminists came from out of the only place they could have come—the housewives of the world!* . . . Satisfaction (for the housewife) lies in allowing and encouraging men to freely assume more and more equal relationship with their children and their wives.[38]

Silences and Decisions

Once again, Lorraine saw things differently from those around her. Despite her mother's urging and the marriages of her older sister and her friends, she knew she did not want to be a housewife. Indeed, she questioned the familiar values about sexuality and the widely accepted ideas of what it meant to be a woman.

Still, Hansberry felt very deeply for Robert Nemiroff, and their time together was fulfilling. They shared values

The Second Sex

"[Hansberry] was, it is clear, an early and lucid [clearthinking] feminist. In 1957, she had begun the draft of an essay on Simone de Beauvoir's *The Second Sex* in which [she] said, '*The Second Sex* may well be the most important work of this century.' She assessed the reception of the book in America, the gossip surrounding de Beauvoir's personal life which substituted for serious debate on her ideas. In the course of this essay, she addressed the politics of housework, pornography (which she recognized immediately as a feminist issue), women's work outside the home, the politics of dress and adornment, the socialist position regarding women's role, and much else that the late 1960s wave of feminism was to address as if for the first time."

and interests. He supported her writing and her activism. If she were to marry, many things would be settled. She could get on with what was important to her—her work.

Finally, she acknowledged how important Nemiroff was to her and decided to marry him. While at home in Chicago for Christmas in 1952, she wrote to Nemiroff, back in New York. Dissatisfied with the letter, she ripped it up and began again. This time she mailed it:

Chicago
December 26, 1952

My Dear Bob,
Once again I wrote you a very long letter—the important simple things which it said were that I have finally admitted to myself that I *do* love you; it

said I have a terrific, no, exciting idea for a play. . . . I am returning to New York, the most important thing about this trip being the long train ride here which cleared my head so that for the first time I thought certain things through to some basic conclusions. They go thusly:
First about "my work":
1. I am a writer. I am going to write.[39]

Hansberry's complicated life was divided by many demands. Her desires were complex and sometimes conflicting. Marriage to Nemiroff would provide Lorraine with a safe harbor. From there she could venture forth in her work for black rights, or she could retreat from the world, immersing herself in her writing.

Chapter

4 Devoting Herself to Her Work

On June 20, 1953, Lorraine Hansberry and Robert Nemiroff married in her mother's home in Chicago among a crowd of family and friends. In many ways this was to be a very untraditional marriage. On the night before the wedding, Lorraine and Robert took part in a demonstration protesting the execution of Julius and Ethel Rosenberg, a Jewish-American couple who had been convicted of espionage, specifically of passing atomic secrets to the Communists. This marriage marked the beginning of a period that combined family and theater with political activities. The two of them moved into a Greenwich Village apartment above Joe's Hand Laundry.

Lorraine quit her job as a full-time journalist with *Freedom* in 1953 and began to devote herself to personal writing projects, her novel, and several different plays that were swimming in her head.

In 1954 she wrote a pageant of the history of the black press's work for equal rights. It was presented at Harlem's Rockland Palace to raise money for *Freedom*.

She took a series of part-time jobs and contributed articles to *Freedom* until it went out of business in 1955. Then she worked as a typist and a secretary, quitting one job after learning that her main role was to serve the coffee. She wrote for a folk mag-

azine, *Sing Out*, working with Pete Seeger, the magazine's cofounder. The well-known folksinger was committed to many of the same causes backed by Lorraine

Lorraine Hansberry and Robert Nemiroff pose with their wedding cake. After the marriage, Hansberry devoted herself to writing full-time.

and wrote such songs as "If I Had a Hammer" and "Where Have All the Flowers Gone?" For a while she was an associate editor for a left-wing magazine for teenagers, *New Challenge*. She reported on NAACP youth conferences, the history of the Jim Crow system, and the death of Emmett Till, who had been a Chicago resident before being lynched in Mississippi. In a series on "Heroes of the New South" she wrote about people like Autherine Lucy, who was the first black student to attend the University of Alabama, as well as participants in the Montgomery bus boycott and white students working in the South to end segregation.

1956—A Big Year

While Lorraine was writing and working odd jobs, Robert worked as a reader and copywriter for Sears Readers Club and then as promotions director of Avon Books. In 1956, after three years of marriage, Robert got together with an old college friend, Burt D'Lugoff, who shared the couple's interest in folk music. Together, the two men wrote a popular song, and Lorraine came up with the title, "Cindy, Oh, Cindy." To everyone's surprise and pleasure it became a big hit. The disc jockeys began playing it on the radio, and before it was displaced by newer material, the song had earned them $100,000. It also provided Robert with a new job at a music publishing firm run by his friend Philip Rose.

Suddenly, there was enough money to pay all the bills, and Lorraine was freed from the part-time jobs. She sat down at her typewriter chain-smoking and drinking coffee, and began to work.

Often she wrote far into the night. At first she worked on her novel, several

News reporters photograph a black student attempting to enroll at the University of Alabama. Blacks continued to challenge racism in education.

Friends and songwriters Robert Nemiroff (left) and Burt D'Lugoff (right). When the duo's song "Cindy, Oh, Cindy" became a hit, Lorraine and Robert achieved a degree of financial stability.

plays, and an opera about her childhood hero, Toussaint L'Ouverture, the liberator of Haiti. Gradually, she found herself concentrating on one play into which she poured her own most painful experiences: her family's fight for equal housing, the devastating effects of prejudice, and the death of her father.

The black family in her play, *A Raisin in the Sun*, grew up, as she had, on the South Side of Chicago. The parents, like her own, had come north searching for a better life. But this family was not well off, as her own had been. Rather, it was more like the families she had admired so much as a child: poor but hardworking and courageous.

A Raisin in the Sun begins after the father's death with the Younger family in conflict. They cannot agree on what to do with the $10,000 life insurance policy left to them. In spite of his death, the father's

values and his memory are very much alive. Lena voices her husband's belief in education and hard work. She wants to use the money to help her daughter, Beneatha, with college and to buy a home in a better area, escaping the ghetto.

Lena's son, Walter Lee, wants to buy a liquor store with the money. He's tired of his dead-end job as a chauffeur. The play centers on the conflict between Lena's traditional values and Walter Lee's dream of material success.

When Lena buys a house in a white neighborhood, Walter Lee's hopes are shattered. Feeling powerless, he quits his job and spends his days drinking.

By the end of the play, Walter Lee has changed. When a white neighbor comes over to try to convince Lena to sell him the house Walter Lee throws the neighbor out. Walter Lee comes to believe that he has earned the right to live where he

Actors Claudia McNeil (left) and Sidney Poitier (right) portray Lena and Walter Lee in a scene from A Raisin in the Sun.

wants because of the sacrifices made by his father and previous generations. He values himself as a black man and gives up his goals of material success.

Hansberry's Feminist Vision

A Raisin in the Sun is as complicated as Hansberry's own life. Her main concern was racism, but the play contains a strong thread of feminism, as well. Lorraine filled the stage with the kinds of problems that turn women into feminists. Showing their independence, her characters rebel against situations that confine and limit them. They speak out on controversial issues. The goal of Beneatha, the young daughter in the play, is to be independent, to become a doctor. Trapping a "breadwinner" is not important, being the best that she can be is what she strives for. Her sister-in-law, Ruth, works as a maid and is

considering an abortion. Ruth and her husband, Walter Lee, cannot afford another child in their crowded ghetto apartment, and Ruth does not want to put more strain on her rocky marriage. Abortion was an important issue for poor people, especially in the 1950s, when the operation was illegal in the United States.

Hansberry brings up feminist concerns in black marriages. For example, Walter Lee blames his problems on the women in his family. He'd be successful if he only had some support.

"That is just what is wrong with the colored woman in this world," Walter Lee complains. "Don't understand about building their men up and making 'em feel like they somebody. Like they can do something. . . . We one group of men tied to a race of women with small minds!"[40]

Professor Sharon Friedman of New York University, writing about feminist plays, sees Hansberry's feminism in the way she presents black family relations:

Feminism Demands Change

In a letter printed in the Ladder, *a lesbian publication, Hansberry argued that every part of American life must change. She felt that educated, determined women must bring this change about, since she saw women's role as less-than-man as the basis of society's fear of homosexuals.*

"It is time that 'half the human race' had something to say about the nature of its existence. Otherwise—without revised basic thinking—the woman intellectual is likely to find herself trying to draw conclusions—moral conclusions—based on acceptance of a social moral superstructure which has never admitted to the equality of women and is therefore immoral itself. As per marriage, as per sexual practices, as per the rearing of children, etc.

In this kind of work there may be women to emerge who will be able to formulate a new and possible concept that homosexual persecution and condemnation has at its roots not only social ignorance, but a philosophically active anti-feminist dogma."

In the play A Raisin in the Sun, *Hansberry explored the roles and frustrations of black women.*

The condition of women forced to work at subsistence wages . . . is epitomized [shown] by Hansberry in her portrayal of the black domestic who must clean the kitchens of white women as well as her own. At the same time, she is expected to bolster the male ego which has been deflated by racism and poverty. . . . Because of their urgency to move the family out of the ghetto, they are vulnerable to Walter's accusation . . . of "not thinking big enough" and of frustrating men's ambitions. Hansberry's answer is that the ghetto kills, not only . . . dreams . . . but the bodies of the children Ruth must feed or abort.[41]

Lena, the mother, is a central character in the play. She is the family's strength and its pride. Lena helps her son connect to the generations of ordinary men and women who fought for their dignity. It is through her that he finds a new way to be a man. Hansberry, in a speech, pinpointed Lena's importance:

> Lena Younger, the mother, is the black matriarch incarnate; the bulwark of the Negro family since slavery, the embodiment of the Negro will to transcendence. It is she who, in the mind of the black poet, scrubs the floors of the nation in order to create black diplomats and university professors. Seemingly clinging to tradition . . . it is she who drives the young into the fire hoses. And one day she simply refuses to move to the back of the bus in Montgomery, and goes out and buys a house in an all white neighborhood where her children may possibly be killed by bricks thrown through the windows by a shrieking racist mob. I'm saying that the mother wins the triumphant moment.[42]

Producing a Play

For eight months Lorraine went each day to a small back room in the apartment to work and rework her play. She found writing to be a solitary and sometimes discouraging task. On one occasion when nothing was going right, Lorraine threw her pages onto the floor in disgust. Nemiroff said nothing, just quietly collected the scattered papers and removed them from her sight. Later, when she was moodily walking about the apartment with nothing to do, he handed her the neatly stacked pages. She took them to her desk and returned to work.

Eventually, the words came easier. She wrote about the end of this difficult period in a postscript to a letter:

> P.S.—The truth is much of it *is* labored —much, however, reads well—and for the first time begins to approximate what I thought I wanted to say. Above

---

Beneatha Is Me

During an interview, Studs Terkel asked Hansberry about Beneatha, the young feminist character, from A Raisin in the Sun.

"Terkel: The very charming and lively little sister—is she slightly autobiographical?

Hansberry: Oh, she's *very* autobiographical! [laughing.] My sister, my brother would tell you that! The truth of the matter is that I enjoyed making fun of this girl who is myself eight years ago. I have great confidence about what she represents. She doesn't have a word in the play that I don't agree with still, today. I would say it differently today."

Claudia McNeil plays Lena, one of the central characters in A Raisin in the Sun. *Hansberry credited Lena, the matriarch of the Younger family, as being "the bulwark of the Negro family."*

all—I am beginning to think of the [characters in the play] *as people. . . .* I talk to them now and all that sort of thing. I am either cracking or turning into a fugging genius. You decide.[43]

By the fall of 1957 the final draft of *A Raisin in the Sun* was finished. Lorraine thought it was good. So did Robert. They decided to have a small dinner party and read the play to their friend Burt D'Lugoff and Robert's boss, music publisher Philip Rose. Their first audience was enthusiastic. The two guests loved the play, discussing the plot and characters late into the night. As a result, Philip Rose accepted the major undertaking of producing the play.

Overcoming Obstacles

Lorraine was pleased but amazed that things were happening so fast. Rose had no experience producing plays, but he did have a good business sense and a belief in *A Raisin in the Sun*. The biggest obstacle was money. Broadway producers Rose approached did not think a dramatic play about blacks could be successful. No black drama had done well on Broadway since Langston Hughes's play *Mulatto*, back in 1935. No one expected a repeat of that success from this young, unknown black woman. It took most of a year for Rose to find backers, people who were willing to invest small amounts in the production. Black cultural leaders like Harry Belafonte, the popular actor and calypso singer, took a chance on the play, as did many others. By the year's end there were more investors for Lorraine's play than any production that had ever appeared on Broadway. At last they could begin.

The subject matter of the play, too, was an obstacle, for realistic plays were not popular at that time. The trend, instead, was toward plays in which the action is disconnected and deliberately confusing: the theater of the absurd. Literature scholar Steven Carter compares absurdist works to a dramatic jigsaw puzzle in which the pieces do not fit together, a crazy quilt pattern supposedly showing that life has no

This Complex of Womanhood

In a feminist essay for Ebony *in 1960, Hansberry questions stereotyped, romantic images of black women. Modern black womanhood, she says, is complex, defiant, and striving for change.*

"On the one hand the Negro poet has created the image of a figure of supreme tenderness and humanity and dignity; a splendid rock-like foundation of a people. She is saluted as a monument of endurance and fortitude, in whose bosom all comforts reside.

And, at the same time, another legend of the Negro woman describes the most over-conversational, uncooperative, overbearing, humiliating, deprecating [belittling] creature ever placed on earth to plague . . . the male. She is seen as an over-practical, unreasonable source of the destruction of all vision and totally lacking a sense of the proper 'place' of womanhood.

Either image taken alone is romance; put together they . . . present the complex of womanhood which . . . now awakens . . . to find itself . . . bound to the world's most insurgent elements. . . . [I]n the United States, a seamstress refuses one day, simply refuses, to move from her chosen place on a bus while an equally remarkable sister of hers ushers children past bayonets in Little Rock. It is indeed a single march, a unified destiny, and the prize is the future. . . . [I]n behalf of an ailing world which surely needs our defiance, may we, as Negroes or *women* never accept the notion of 'our place.' "

meaning. Absurdist playwrights like Samuel Beckett and Edward Albee characterized life as irrational in an outrageous, incomprehensible way—that is, absurd. In their plays, nothing could be depended on, not even God, because God did not exist, and therefore, action was pointless.

Although Hansberry was an atheist—that is, she did not believe in God—she strongly disagreed with the absurdist philosophy and its logical conclusion, hopelessness. Like the absurdist playwrights,

she knew that life was uncertain and people sometimes were cruel. She often felt lonely, depressed, and fearful. But, despite what she had seen and experienced of oppression, she believed that society could change. She argued that people would commit themselves to action.

She believed that good art should have a message and urge a cause. In fact, she believed it wasn't possible to create a work of art that didn't make a social statement of some kind. She was an activist who worked for the causes she believed in. She used her art to encourage others to take a stand, to make a difference.

"The human race does command its own destiny and that destiny can embrace the stars,"[44] she said. She spoke about these issues only two weeks before the Broadway opening of *A Raisin in the Sun*. Her name was becoming known, and she had been asked to address a black writers' conference. In her speech she argued that blacks must take part in the struggles going on in society. She said that an artist's creation should make a political statement. The speech was her ethic and she challenged others to join her:

> I persist in the simple view that all art is ultimately social: that which agitates and that which prepares the mind for slumber. The writer is deceived who thinks that he has some other choice. The question is not whether one will make a social statement in one's work—but only *what* the statement will say, for if it says anything at all, it will be social.[45]

In conclusion she told a story:

> I must share with you now a part of a conversation I had with a young New York intellectual a year ago in my living room in Greenwich Village. . . . "Why," he said to me, "are you so sure the human race *should* go on? You do not believe in prior arrangement of life on this planet. You know perfectly well that the *reason* for survival does not exist in nature!"

> I answered him the only way I could. I argued on his own terms, which are also mine: That man is unique in the universe, the only creature who has in

fact the power to transform the universe. Therefore, it did not seem unthinkable to me that man might just do what the apes never will—*impose the reason for life on life.*[46]

Overcoming More Obstacles

While Philip Rose was busy lining up backers, the search for actors and a director was proceeding, as well. Sidney Poitier, an unknown film actor and an acquaintance of Lorraine's, was contacted and he fell under the play's spell. Poitier recommended

Sidney Poitier agreed to play Lena's son Walter Lee in A Raisin in the Sun. *He also recommended a director for the play.*

his teacher, Lloyd Richards, as a director. Although Richards's name was not familiar to Hansberry and Rose, they were impressed with the man himself. If the play made it to Broadway, Richards would be Broadway's first black director.

Another obstacle was locating a theater that would take on the play. Theater owners didn't want to hire out their buildings unless they felt a play would have a long and successful run. *A Raisin in the Sun* was a gamble, and no Broadway theater could be found. Rose began by booking out-of-town houses. If the venture was successful in New Haven, Philadelphia, and Chicago, good reviews might convince a Broadway theater to take a chance.

When the company moved to New Haven for the first opening, Hansberry was excited but nervous. So many people's salaries depended on how well her play did. Would the audiences like it? From her hotel room in New Haven, she wrote a letter to her mother.

> Hotel Taft
> New Haven, Connecticut
> January 19, 1959
>
> Dear Mother,
> Well—here we are. I am sitting alone in a nice hotel room in New Haven, Conn. Downstairs, next door in the Shubert Theatre, technicians are putting the finishing touches on a living room that is supposed to be a Chicago living room. Wednesday the curtain goes up at 8 P.M. The next day the New Haven papers will say what they think about our efforts. A great deal of money has been spent and a lot of people have done some hard, hard work, and it may be the beginning of many different careers.

The actors are very good and the director is a very talented man—so if it is a poor show I won't be able to blame a soul but your youngest daughter.

Mama, it is a play that tells the truth about people, Negroes and life and I think it will help a lot of people to understand how we are just as complicated as they are—and just as mixed up—but above all, that we have among our miserable and downtrodden ranks—people who are the very essence of human dignity. That is what, after all the laughter and tears, the play is supposed to say. I hope it will make you very proud. See you soon. Love to all.[47]

An eager Hansberry awaits the New Haven opening of A Raisin in the Sun.

The Philadelphia Opening

On Raisin *'s twenty-fifth anniversary, the writer James Baldwin discussed the play's appeal to the black community in Philadelphia. The article appeared in the magazine* American Theatre.

James Baldwin praised Raisin *for its impact on the black community.*

"Lorraine and I met in Philadelphia, in 1959, when *A Raisin in the Sun* was at the beginning of its amazing career. Much has been written about this play: I personally feel that it will demand a far less guilty and constricted people than the present-day Americans to be able to assess it at all; as an historical achievement, anyway, no one can gainsay [deny] its importance. What is relevant here is that I had never in my life seen so many black people in the theatre. And the reason was that never before, in the entire history of the American theatre, had so much of the truth of black people's lives been seen on the stage. Black people ignored the theatre because the theatre had always ignored them.

But, in *Raisin*, black people recognized that house and all the people in it—the mother, the son, the daughter and the daughter-in-law, and supplied the play with an interpretative element which could not be present in the minds of white people: a kind of claustrophobic terror, created not only by their knowledge of the house but by their knowledge of the streets."

The trial run at New Haven was a success. The reviews were complimentary, and audiences seemed to understand what Hansberry was trying to say. Some even recognized the influence of Sean O'Casey, the Irish playwright.

The production in Philadelphia was also well received, but because the work was not well known yet, it often played to half-empty houses. The future was still uncertain, but Richards continued to search for a Broadway theater. Then he had an experience that convinced him the play was gaining momentum. He was standing in front of the Philadelphia theater when a small black woman, evidently a domestic worker, carrying her work shoes in a bag, approached the box office. He asked her courteously what she was doing there. She responded solemnly that the word was going round in her neighborhood that something was happening at the theater that concerned her. Later in his career, *Raisin*'s first director often told of this happy moment when he realized that news of the play was reaching the black community.

The good Philadelphia reviews led Shubert-owned theaters to finance a move to Chicago and then to the Ethel Barrymore Theatre on Broadway. The company was jubilant. They had their house on Broadway!

Opening in Chicago was a thrill for Lorraine. She felt proud of herself, coming back to her hometown a successful writer. She was pleased to give something back to the city that produced her vision. The Chicago critics liked her play, and the audiences were enthusiastic, but even this success did nothing to decrease Hansberry's anxiety. New York would determine the play's fate.

Opening Night on Broadway

The company approached the Broadway opening with anxiety. If the reviews were not good, it could still fail. If they were complimentary, tickets would sell quickly and success was ensured. March 11, 1959, *A Raisin in the Sun* opened, pleasing critics and audiences alike. Everything worked. The cast, led by Sidney Poitier as Walter Lee and Claudia McNeil as the mother, was strong and exciting. The audience cheered at the final curtain, drawing the actors out for curtain call after curtain call. Suddenly, Poitier jumped from the stage to catch Lorraine's hand, pulling her up to join the cast in receiving the applause. Applause for what she had begun to create alone in her room one and a half years earlier. Bringing the play to Broadway had been a long hard job, an unlikely project with little chance of success, but they had done it. *A Raisin in*

A poster advertises the production of A Raisin in the Sun *at the Barrymore Theatre. The play was a hit on Broadway, earning the respect of critics and audiences.*

the Sun was an immediate hit, breaking new ground in the theater with a serious black drama exploring racism.

The Time Had Come

Broadway's ready acceptance of *A Raisin in the Sun* was surprising, since it had been so difficult to fund the play and place it in a theater. No one had expected this level of success. Most people were not aware that

1959 was the right time for such a work: Five years had elapsed since the Supreme Court decision in *Brown* v. *Topeka Board of Education* had resulted in the desegregation of the nation's public schools, and it had been four years since the bus boycott initiated by Rosa Parks in Montgomery, Alabama. Attitudes were changing.

Historian Lerone Bennett Jr. explained Hansberry's role: "She was a kind of herald, a person announcing the coming of something. It was in the air, I think, and whites felt it as well as Blacks."[48]

Hansberry's play catches the essence of the early civil rights struggle. It is about equal rights in work and in housing, and about the freedom movement of the past. In the first half of the twentieth century, the fight for black rights was conducted through legal channels in the courts and through advocacy, not confrontation. After WWII, which saw the end of colonialism throughout the world, a new radicalism marked the struggle for black freedom in the United States. In the context of the late 1950s, Hansberry's play announced the coming of a new kind of struggle. The black sit-ins at the Woolworth lunch counters in North Carolina began in 1960, launching a more forceful attack on segregated public spaces. A new black militancy, symbolized by the slogan "Black power," would follow with the rise to prominence of Malcolm X, whom Hansberry knew and supported.

Few, however, recognized the militancy and revolutionary tone of the play. When *A Raisin in the Sun* opened, militant blacks, like the author LeRoi Jones, who took the name Amiri Baraka, dismissed Hansberry and her play, which he said was too passive and middle class. Yet in 1986, when the play was restaged to enthusiastic audiences at its twenty-fifth anniversary, Baraka and many others saw it in the light of the civil rights movement that had flowered soon after the original production. With a new appreciation for Hansberry's work, Baraka admitted that earlier he had missed the play's essence. He now felt the play marked the point when the power was passed from the old freedom movement to the young radicals of the civil rights era. He said:

Black college students engage in a sit-in at a Woolworth lunch counter in North Carolina to protest Woolworth's policy of not serving blacks.

The Director Looks Back

Director Lloyd Richards looks back on the many obstacles overcome by A Raisin in the Sun *in an* American Theatre *article celebrating the silver anniversary of the play's opening.*

"When I consider how close that play came to not being produced, I am stunned. . . . It took more than a year to raise the money. There were more investors in *A Raisin in the Sun* than in any production that had ever appeared on Broadway. The biggest investment was $750; the average was $250—little people who believed in an idea, the naive first-time investor who had not yet been educated to understand what was impossible. Several times the project was almost jettisoned. We approached the rehearsal date in September without capitalization. Unfortunately, but luckily for us, the set of the movie that Sidney [Poitier] was working on burned down, so we were able to postpone rehearsals until December while they built a new set and finished the movie. We finally went into rehearsal in New York, after which we had scheduled four days of playing in New Haven, one week in Philadelphia with a total advance sale of $600, and no New York theatre to open in. It could all have ended in Philadelphia. Any knowledgeable person would have known you couldn't have done it. *We* didn't know any better. We had no choice.

The rest is history. We relished the triumph and the Cinderella aspect of that production. However, it is important that we remember how close it came to not happening at all."

Lloyd Richards (right) directs Sidney Poitier and Claudia McNeil in a scene from A Raisin in the Sun.

The concerns I once dismissed as "middle class"—buying a house and moving into "white folks' neighborhoods"—are actually reflective of the essence of black people's striving and the will to defeat segregation, discrimination, and national oppression. There is no such thing as a "white folks' neighborhood" except to racists *and to those submitting to racism.*

The Younger family is the incarnation—*before* they burst from the bloody Southern backroads and the burning streets of Watts and Newark onto TV screens and the *world* stage—of our common ghetto-variety Fanny Lou Hamers [sharecroppers turned activists], Malcolm X's and Angela Davises [college professor turned revolutionary leader]. And their burden surely will be lifted, or one day it certainly will "explode."[49]

Hansberry's play spoke not only to blacks, it had a message for whites who knew little about the black community that existed in their midst. Many whites were learning what was happening there as they watched television news clips of the use of fire hoses, police attack dogs, and beatings against peaceful demonstrators in the South. These viewers were a ready audience for a play about the black struggle. As biographer Margaret Wilkerson wrote, Hansberry "captured the heroism and frustration of a whole era and the heart of a divided nation."[50]

Changing the Face of American Theater

The impact of Hansberry's play was profound. It influenced all succeeding generations of black theater artists. On April 7, 1959, Hansberry was given the award for best play of the year by the New York Drama Critics Circle.

Lorraine was the first black writer to ever win this important honor. At twenty-nine she was also the youngest writer to receive it and only the fifth woman. Not only did *A Raisin in the Sun* make Nannie Hansberry proud, as Lorraine had hoped when she wrote her mother before the New Haven opening, the play became an

Police turn fire hoses on protesters during an anti-segregation rally. Here, three demonstrators hold hands to withstand the force of the water.

(Left) In 1959 Lorraine Hansberry won the New York Drama Critics Circle award for the best play of the year. (Top) The Barrymore was quick to place the award on its advertisements for A Raisin in the Sun.

American classic. It has been translated into thirty languages and produced in countries as far away as France and Russia. It has been performed by thousands of theater groups and turned into a movie, an American Playhouse television play, and a musical. In a 1986 review of American theater, the *Washington Post* called *A Raisin in the Sun* one of a handful of great dramas to capture American life. It was grouped with Arthur Miller's *Death of a Salesman*, Eugene O'Neill's *Long Day's Journey into Night*, and Tennessee Williams's *The Glass Menagerie*.

The impact of *Raisin* on black artists, actors, and playwrights was revolutionary. It began a deluge of work: realistic plays and stories about black lives. Hansberry's success encouraged black artists to try. Clearly it could be done. Typical of the respect paid the play are the words of scholar David Littlejohn: "It would not be unfair in dating the emergence of a serious and mature Negro theatre in America from 1959, the date of Lorraine Hansberry's *A Raisin in the Sun.*"[51]

Because of this, Hansberry is referred to as the mother of modern black drama.

5 Misunderstandings

Despite the success of *A Raisin in the Sun*, audiences and certain critics at times misunderstood the play. What most upset Lorraine was the suggestion by some critics that the Youngers, her black family, were too white. From the other side of the issue, there were those who dismissed the play as nothing but propaganda to support integration. These negative views were disappointing to Lorraine, who wanted to write a black play. She wanted to honestly portray a black family's life in all its variety. She wanted to show their particular language and culture; their courage in resisting racism. She had no intention of delivering a message for integrated housing; she wanted to show the strength of blacks who were fighting racism and to question American materialism.

The allegation that she was "whitening" her black family was encouraged by newspaper reporters who misquoted Lorraine even before the play opened. Nan Robertson, of the *New York Times*, quoted Lorraine as saying, "This wasn't a 'Negro play.' It was a play about honest-to-God believable, many sided people who happened to be Negroes."[52]

Hansberry had not said, "This wasn't a 'Negro play,'" and she protested in a heated exchange of letters, demanding that Robertson admit her error. The con-

Hansberry aspired to make A Raisin in the Sun *an honest portrayal of black life, and she was extremely disappointed when critics claimed that her characters were too white.*

fusion was never cleared up, however, because the desired correction was never published.

Hansberry protested because the misquote expressed the very opposite of her philosophy that black playwrights should "write about our people, tell their story."[53]

She tried without success to correct the misunderstanding in later interviews. In a radio interview two months after the play opened, when Studs Terkel asked Lorraine what she would say to someone who claimed *A Raisin in the Sun* was not a black play, that it could be about anyone, she replied:

> I have told people that not only is this a Negro family, specifically and culturally, but it's not even a New York family or a southern Negro family—it is specifically Southside Chicago. To the extent we accept them and believe them as who they're supposed to be, to that extent they can become everybody. So I would say it is definitely a Negro play before it is anything else.[54]

While Lorraine was intent on telling the story of her people, she would not allow herself to be limited to this subject alone. During her life she wrote about many different times and cultures: slavery and the Civil War, modern Africa, Chicago and Greenwich Village, the Haiti of Toussaint L'Ouverture, the eighteenth-century England of early feminist Mary Wollstonecraft, the Egypt of the pharaohs, and the life of Southwest Navajos in the early 1900s.

Nor would Hansberry be confined to narrow labels. While she was proud of her identities—"black woman," "black playwright," "realistic playwright"—scholar Steven Carter writes that Lorraine "could never be exclusively defined by them. Each time she juggled these qualities with

A Universal Appreciation

In an interview published in the magazine Freedomways, *historian Lerone Bennett discusses Hansberry as a universal playwright.*

"From my reading of Lorraine Hansberry, I get the feeling that she struggled all her life with the whole question of 'universality.' And I interpret her as having struggled against *false* definitions of 'universality.' I consider her a black playwright who wrote a classic play. . . . An artist is most universal when [s]he's discussing the concrete issues of . . . [her] own culture. It's the task of the artist to take the concrete and make it universal. What I'm saying here is that people try to say, well, you know if X wrote a play about black people, she's not universal. But if an Irish playwright writes a play about Irish people, he's universal. So the play is about black people—black people *are* human. She wrote a play which is a classic, and which speaks to the human condition, not only the condition of black people. But I consider her a black playwright as I consider O'Casey an Irish playwright. She was universal in her particularity."

their supposed opposites, she struck a blow for her own freedom and for the freedom, not only of other artists, but of other human beings."[55]

Rejections

After the success of her play, Hansberry worked on a series of projects. One was writing a screenplay for *Raisin*. Indeed, she had refused to sell the film rights until Columbia Pictures agreed to allow her to write the screenplay. She believed that only this could guarantee that the Younger family would not be turned into Hollywood stereotypes of urban black people.

She was interested in the challenge of translating material written to be produced live on a stage into a movie. The freedom to take her characters out of their three-room apartment and put them into the streets would allow her to show more of the black community and help a white audience understand blacks' everyday encounters with racism. A movie would show what a play could only talk about.

Hansberry wanted to add scenes of Lena Younger struggling with her employer, as well as being exploited and treated rudely by a white grocery clerk. A camera could follow Walter Lee to his dead-end job and through the bustling city that would not give him a chance. Hansberry also wanted to include a street scene in which a black activist uses Walter Lee's own arguments to work up a crowd. The camera would show a stark contrast as Lena and Walter returned home on a streetcar from the wealthy suburbs where they worked, to the ghetto where they were obliged to live.

Some members of the theater audience had assumed that the family's move to a new neighborhood was a "happy ending," that all the black family wanted was to live among whites. This misinterpretation reflected not only ignorance of what was going on in the real world when such moves were attempted, but also failure to grasp the significance of several lines in the play that emphasized the danger of the move.

A screenplay, on the other hand, could make clear the dangers awaiting the Youngers by having the camera follow the family on a visit to the new neighborhood. Thus in the movie script, Lorraine intended to eliminate any chance that the play would be misunderstood as propaganda for integration. For example, she wanted the camera to show rather ordinary houses revealing

> something sinister. . . . At some windows curtains drop quickly back into place, as though those who are watching do not want to be seen; at others, shadowy figures simply move back out of view when they feel that Walter and Ruth's gaze is upon them; at still others, those who are staring do so without apology. The faces—the eyes of women and children, in the main— look hard with a curiosity that, for the most part, is clearly hostile.[56]

Columbia Pictures felt the added material was too controversial, and would offend the white audiences they were hoping to attract to the film. Therefore, most of the encounters with whites were cut out. Hansberry reworked the screenplay three times, ending with a version that closely resembled the original play.

While the movie version was not what Hansberry had intended, it was still a mile-

A movie still from the 1961 film A Raisin in the Sun. *The play's success on Broadway prompted Hollywood producers to ask Hansberry to write a script for a movie version of the play.*

stone. She was the first black woman to write a Hollywood movie; and her script, with its social criticism, was a unique Hollywood film. Judges of the 1961 Cannes Film Festival gave it the Gary Cooper Award for "outstanding human values," for its depiction of a black family's courageous fight against racism.

The Drinking Gourd

Lorraine continued to work with other media besides the stage. In 1959 she was hired to write a script for the first of a series of television shows for the National Broadcasting Company. The series, intended to dramatize the issues that were part of the Civil War, was scheduled to be aired in 1961, the centennial of the start of the war.

The Drinking Gourd was to be the first television play to explore the institution of slavery: how it affected poor whites and wealthy slave owners as well as black slaves. The title comes from a spiritual used during the days of the Underground Railroad. The term "the drinking gourd" symbolized the Big Dipper constellation, which points to the North Star. Because escaped slaves could follow the North Star to nonslave states and eventual freedom, slaves sang the song to pass information on the escape route. Thus, the song could be sung openly to convey a secret message that slaves would understand, but its meaning would be concealed from white slave owners.

Although producer Dore Schary gave Hansberry complete artistic freedom, problems existed from the very beginning. When the producer told a roomful of television executives that he had a contract with Lorraine Hansberry, the award-winning young black playwright, he was not encouraged by their response. Some time afterward, Schary reported the reaction to Hansberry in the following terms:

There was a long moment of silence. And then the question was asked: "What's her point of view about it—slavery?"

I thought they were pulling my leg, and so I answered presently, gravely: "She's against it."

Nobody laughed—and from that moment I knew we were dead.[57]

It was clear that differing goals were at stake, but Schary was not afraid of controversy. Like Hansberry, he wanted to make a dramatic statement about an evil system. A primary concern for the network executives, on the other hand, was to avoid offending anyone.

Schary did not tell Lorraine about the possibility of problems down the line, and she began her research. She visited the New York Public Library's Schomburg Center for Research in Black Culture in Harlem. She read transcripts of the *Congressional Record* dating back to the Civil War. She studied sermons and speeches of that time, read old diaries, and found newspaper stories of slave rebellions. Lorraine hunted up slavery auction notices, bills of sale for slaves, and wanted posters for runaways.

Hansberry wanted to learn everything she could about life in the time of slavery so that her characters would be believable and the story historically accurate. To an interviewer asking about her research she explained: "What I think a dramatist has to do is to thoroughly inundate . . . herself

The Rejected Screenplay

Three decades after the movie was made, Hansberry's original script was published. For director Spike Lee, reading the version originally submitted was like a revelation. In an introduction to A Raisin in the Sun: The Unfilmed Original Screenplay, *the young black filmmaker writes:*

"Lorraine Hansberry was a visionary. . . . Her play is a landmark in American theater, and in the right hands, the film could have been a landmark in cinema. . . . After I finished reading the screenplay, I went out and rented the video cassette. It seems to me all the cuts had to deal with softening a too defiant black voice. I found the parts that were cut to be some of the most interesting parts of the screenplay. . . .

You might ask, what would Hansberry have done if she hadn't been taken away from us so soon? I'd like to think that *Raisin* would have been her first of many fine screenplays. Can you name another African American female who has written a screenplay for a Hollywood studio that got made? I cannot."

in . . . the realities of the historical period and then dismiss it. And then become absolutely dedicated to the idea that what you are going to do is create human beings whom you know in your own time."[58]

Not for Family Viewing

In *The Drinking Gourd*, Hiram, a plantation owner, dies pleading for help from his slave, Rissa. She turns her back on him, choosing instead to nurse her own son, Hannibal, recently blinded on the orders of Hiram's son, Everett, as punishment for the crime of learning to read. Hannibal had intended to begin a new life in the North, and now he needs Rissa's help to execute his plan. As Hannibal makes his escape, Everett is seen joining the Confederate army in the struggle to preserve slavery. Viewers understand that Everett is destined to die in battle.

In the end the play was paid for, a note was attached by a television executive calling it superb, and then it was put away in a drawer never to be produced. NBC considered it too violent and controversial for family viewing. Dore Schary lost his contract and left television. Commenting on network TV's timidity in presenting a full picture of slavery, Schary told a reporter "I want no part of this nonsense."[59]

The Blacks and *The Whites*

Hansberry had begun work on another play in the summer of 1960, but it had not progressed very far. It was about the liberation of Africans from colonial rule.

One evening she saw the American premier of *Les Negres* (*The Blacks*), a very successful play by the French playwright Jean Genet. Lorraine was angry and upset by the play because it did the very thing she hated—stereotyped blacks. It portrayed blacks as exotic, as different from whites. It said nothing about real black lives.

In Genet's highly symbolic play, a group of bizarrely dressed black actors give a performance in which they are on trial for the rape and murder of a white woman. The accused act out the crime before a fantastic jury (a queen, a general, a judge, and a missionary), who are played by black actors wearing white masks. During the trial a revolution between whites and blacks is raging offstage. In the end the accused con-

Dore Schary hired Lorraine Hansberry to write a television play about the Civil War. Despite Schary's support, Hansberry's play The Drinking Gourd *was never produced.*

The Controversial *Drinking Gourd*

In a 1961 radio discussion, "Negro Writer in America," Hansberry talked with James Baldwin, Langston Hughes, Alfred Kazin, Nat Hentoff, and Emile Capouya about her experience trying to write about the Civil War and slavery.

"We've been trying very hard . . . in America to pretend that this greatest conflict didn't even have at its base the only thing it had at its base: where person after person will write a book today and insist that *slavery* was not the issue! You know, they tell you it was the 'economy'—as if that economy was not based on slavery. It's become a great semantic game to try and get this particular blot out of our minds, and people spend volumes discussing the *battles* of the Civil War, and which army was crossing which river at five minutes to two, and how their swords were hanging, but the slavery issue we have tried to get rid of. To a point that while it has been perfectly popular, admirable, the thing to do—all my life since *Gone with the Wind*—to write anything you wanted about the slave system with beautiful ladies in big, fat dresses screaming as their houses burned down from the terrible, nasty, awful Yankees . . . this has been such a perfectly acceptable part of our culture that the first time that I know of that someone came to *me* and asked me to write ninety minutes of television drama on slavery—which, if you will accept my own estimate, was not a propaganda piece in either direction but, I hope, a serious treatment of family relationships by a slave-owning family and their slaves—*this* is controversial. This has never been done."

demn the "white" judges and leave the stage dancing a strange minuet.

Les Negres helped Hansberry to focus her ideas about the play she was working on. In half-joking reference to Genet's title, she called her play *Les Blancs* (French for *The Whites*). The white author Genet wrote his fanciful, symbolic view of racial revolution and Hansberry wrote hers: a realistic drama of confrontation.

English Colonialism

From her research in connection with the articles for *Freedom* and her studies under Du Bois, Hansberry knew a lot about Africa's history of colonial rule. In writing "Kikuyu: A Peaceful People Wage Heroic Struggle Against British," she learned that for centuries, Britain and other foreign

A group of Kikuyu tribesmen are held as prisoners in Kenya. Hansberry used the rebellion of the Kikuyu against British colonialism as the basis for her play Les Blancs.

powers had moved into Africa, attracted by the fertile land and precious metals. European countries then established colonies and sent their nationals to settle in Africa and act as administrators. In the early 1900s laws were written to keep the African people at the bottom of the economic ladder. In Kenya, for example, large taxes were imposed at the same time that limits were placed on what Africans could grow on their own land. As a result, the people were not able to support themselves.

For thirty years the Kikuyu people tried to get the laws changed by peaceful means. When Jomo Kenyatta, a Kikuyu leader who believed in peace and conciliation, was arrested on the charge of plotting insurrection, the country exploded. Soon Kikuyu terrorist groups, called Mau Maus by the English press, attacked the white colonialists.

Lorraine set her play in Kenya around 1952, the time of the bloody Mau Mau revolt against the British. In *Les Blancs*, she considered the situation of the Africans who killed for freedom. Her play was also a warning. If action was not taken to right the wrong of colonial exploitation, the danger of violent revolution would be ever present. Hansberry biographer Margaret Wilkerson explains that Hansberry was not supporting violence. She was using the theater to explore the consequences of racism and the system of colonialism. Just as in *The Drinking Gourd,* her purposes in

Les Blancs were to show how an oppressive system destroys everyone it touches, to focus on a few individuals responding to their place in history, and to show that people will always strive for freedom.

In *Les Blancs* a well-meaning white American journalist comes to Africa to write the story of a white missionary, Reverend Neilsen, who, we learn, is a racist who looks on the native people as children. Tshembe, a handsome young African, comes home from Europe for his father's funeral, leaving his white wife and their son abroad. He does not want to be involved in his native country's struggle for freedom from the white colonialists. He sees both sides and loves people on both sides of the color lines.

Nevertheless, Tshembe is caught up in his people's struggle. In the end, he shoots his brother, a Catholic priest, who allied himself with the British and betrayed an African underground leader. The Kikuyu revolutionaries attack the mission, and as it explodes in flames the white woman who raised Tshembe, Madame Neilsen, dies in the gunfire. Before the shooting, the journalist leaves Africa to write his book. His eyes have been opened, and the story he will write is different from the one he had expected to file. He goes off, telling Tshembe, "We're on the same side."[60]

Lorraine Hansberry worked on *Les Blancs* for the remainder of her life. She never finished it.

Many Irons in the Fire

Hansberry began another play, a musical she called *The Sign in Jenny Reed's Window*, based on an experience with a Greenwich Village neighbor, Gin Briggs, a woman from the Kentucky hills. Innocently, unaware of local traditions and loyalties, Briggs hung a poster in her window that condemned Carmine Desapio, a powerful New York politician frequently alleged to have connections to organized crime. After the sign went up Briggs was threatened, her windows were smashed, and she was very nearly evicted from her apartment. In *The Sign in Jenny Reed's Window* the main character is moved from apathy to commitment as he takes a stand against drugs and corrupt politics.

Hansberry described the musical as a play that looked at commitment, which she felt was "one of the leading problems before my generation here: what to identify with, what to become involved in; what to take a stand on; what, if you will, even to believe in at all."[61]

Chitterling Heights

By 1961 it was clear there were problems in the marriage of Lorraine Hansberry and Robert Nemiroff. They continued to support each other in their creative lives, but emotionally they went separate ways. Despite the growing fissure, they remained together publicly until 1964, when they quietly received a Mexican divorce.

Regardless of their problems, however, in the summer of 1961 Lorraine and Robert bought a home in Croton-on-Hudson, a quiet, wooded area near the Hudson River an hour away from New York City. Here, in a soundproof study with her desk and three filing cabinets full of projects, Lorraine felt she could concentrate more easily on her writing. She surrounded herself with pictures of human capability. On the wall in front of her desk she hung a photo of Paul Robeson and one of Michelangelo's statue of David, which to her represented the idea of excellence. At her shoulder stood a bust of Einstein, nobility in the flesh. At the top of the stairs hung a picture of Sean O'Casey.

Lorraine called the new residence Chitterling Heights. By using a traditional term for deep-fried hog's intestines as the name of her country estate, she believed she was remembering her southern roots. Despite her personal problems, in Croton she was able to work uninterrupted on her writing. Her journal reflected her happiness.

> Croton-on-Hudson—Chitterling
> Heights!
> August 23, 1962—
>
> Have been here in the country for two weeks. Alone. Herculean [major, difficult] adjustment for me with all my fears. But now feel ready for the struggle. Will work or perish. The air and sky glisten; the wind is crisp. The night is like the beginning of a dream that will reveal the universe, so drenched in lucidity it seems. . . .
>
> What shall I do this year? What shall I become? What shall I learn—truly learn and know that I have learned by the time I look at these pages next year?
>
> These trees! These trees! "Lord, I fear thou didst make the world too beautiful this year.". . . I have felt moods here I had not felt since childhood. They are fleeting and elusive, yes. But they come, praise creation, they come![62]

The Sign in Sidney Brustein's Window

During the hours of writing at her desk at Croton, *The Sign in Jenny Reed's Window* grew and changed from a musical to a drama, becoming *The Sign in Sidney Brustein's Window*. A new main character developed. Jenny Reed changed into Iris, a hopeful actress, and her husband, Sidney, became the center of the play. In the course of the play Sidney grows from a weary intellectual into an activist.

The play is about a group of white intellectuals living in Greenwich Village. *Brustein* is a play of ideas, many ideas and complicated ones about art and politics,

Hansberry in her study at Chitterling Heights. After the move to Croton-on-Hudson, Hansberry began working on the play The Sign in Jenny Reed's Window.

prejudice and homosexuality, marriage and black culture. Hansberry explores the purpose of art and lampoons absurdist plays. She deals with the destructive effects of prejudice against homosexuals, blacks, Jews, and women. She examines marriage, including the need for equality and mutual respect between partners. She investigates the cost of drug addiction to society and especially to blacks; and she questions black nationalism because it isolates the races. The many ideas in the play made it interesting, but some critics found it too complicated, hence confusing.

Brustein was like *Raisin* in one critical way. Both express the values closest to Lorraine's heart: the needs to be committed to a cause, to take one's place in history, and to act. The play, in which Sidney joins in a political campaign to fight drugs in his community, is full of tragedy. Sidney learns that the politician he supports is corrupt; Iris leaves him; one sister-in-law kills herself when her lover rejects her upon learning that she has been a prostitute, and another sister-in-law reveals the emptiness of her marriage with the information that her husband has a son with another woman. Despite all this sadness and betrayal, the play ends with affirmation. Like the Youngers, Sidney will keep going forward. In both plays the people will continue the struggle against injustice. *The Sign in Sidney Brustein's Window* opened on October 15, 1964. It was to be Hansberry's final play.

A Meeting at the Summit

Hansberry continued to be an activist, using her fame as a podium from which to support the black struggle. On May 25, 1963, she was asked to join other black leaders in a meeting with Attorney General Robert F. Kennedy. In an attempt to build bridges and make plans to decrease racial tension, Kennedy had asked Hansberry's friend, author James Baldwin, to set up the meeting.

Baldwin quickly contacted people he felt he could trust: actress and singer Lena Horne, Harry Belafonte, Ed Berry of the Chicago Urban League, black sociologist Dr. Kenneth Clark. Also invited was Jerome Smith, a Congress of Racial Equality activist who had been frequently jailed and beaten during demonstrations but was not, like the others, a well-known representative of black America. Smith became the center of an intense, three-hour confrontation.

Lorraine ended the meeting when she could no longer tolerate the unproductive discussion. As she walked out of the room, the others followed her. The emotional meeting in Kennedy's New York hotel room did not build bridges. Instead, it revealed a deep gulf between the government and the activists. Kennedy would not answer the CORE worker's unrelenting demands for the government to stop the violence against blacks. He turned away from Smith, who was not known to the general public, and tried to engage the celebrities. Lorraine would not allow Smith's demands to be ignored. Her firm admonition is recorded in Baldwin's account of the event, published years later:

"You have a great many very accomplished people in this room, Mr. Attorney General, but the only man you should be listening to is that man over there [Smith]. That is the voice," she

Attorney General Robert Kennedy (left) meets with his brother President John F. Kennedy. In 1963 Lorraine was invited to join James Baldwin and other blacks to speak to Robert F. Kennedy on the subject of racial tension.

added, after a moment during which Bobby sat absolutely still staring at her, "of twenty-two million people." [63]

During the heat of the discussion Lorraine expressed her solidarity with Jerome Smith and the black demonstrators. Speaking for Harry Belafonte, Lena Horne, James Baldwin, and the other famous blacks, she said, "We are not remotely interested in any tea at the White House. What we *are* interested in is in making perfectly clear that between the Negro intelligentsia, the Negro middle class, and the Negro this-and-that—we are *one* people. And that as far as *we* are concerned, we are represented by the Negroes in the streets of Birmingham!" [64]

The Student Nonviolent Coordinating Committee

Determined to support the struggles on the streets, Hansberry took a variety of actions. She helped raise money for civil rights groups by speaking at mass meetings. In 1963 she organized a rally in the town of Croton-on-Hudson to raise money for voter registration in the South. Lorraine spoke in support of Dr. Martin Luther King Jr. and the Southern Christian Leadership Conference.

It would give her both pain and pride to know that the money raised at the rally paid for the station wagon driven by James

Chaney, Michael Schwerner, and Andrew Goodman, who were kidnapped and murdered in 1964 by members of the Ku Klux Klan in Philadelphia, Mississippi. The three activists were in the rural South as participants in Freedom Summer, when young civil rights volunteers, many from northern colleges, came to help organize blacks and register them to vote.

Despite her political work and her playwriting, Lorraine was entering a time of great turmoil and difficulty. Parts of her life that she had thought could remain in the background became harder and harder to silence. Nemiroff stated that her homosexuality "was not a peripheral or casual part of her life, but contributed . . . on many levels to the sensitivity and complexity of her view of human beings and of the world."[65] This identity helped her to see the connection between women's status and discrimination against Jews, blacks, and other ethnic groups; but it also added the burden of secrecy.

To prevent public opinion from labeling and then discrediting her, she felt it was necessary to keep her lesbianism a secret even though it was a large part of her

Sidney Speaks for Lorraine

In the closing speech of The Sign in Sidney Brustein's Window, *Sidney expresses feelings that come from Hansberry's heart. No matter how cruel and unjust the world is, one must commit to action and change. He exclaims to the politician who is threatening him:*

"Don't you understand, man? Too much has happened to me! I love my wife—I want her back. I loved my sister-in-law. I want to see her alive. I—I love you—I should like to see you redeemed. But in the context in which we presently stand here I doubt any of this is possible. That which warped and distorted all of us is—(*Suddenly lifting his hands as if this were literally true*) all around; it is in this very air! *This world*—this swirling, seething madness—which you ask us to accept, to help maintain—has done this . . . maimed my friends . . . emptied these rooms and my very bed. And now it has taken my sister. *This* world! Therefore, to live, to breathe—I shall *have* to fight it!

[The politician calls him a fool and Sidney responds:]

Always have been. (*His eyes find his wife's*) A fool who believes that death is waste and love is sweet and that the earth turns and men change every day and that rivers run and that people wanna be better than they are and that flowers smell good and that I hurt terribly today, and that hurt is desperation and desperation is—energy and energy can move things."

identity. She had to be constantly aware that a part of her life must be camouflaged. The subterfuge may have taken a greater toll than she realized.

Hansberry scholar Steven Carter recognized the isolation this secrecy could create: "Feminist writers . . . have alluded to Hansberry's dilemma as a lesbian in the pre–civil rights, pre–Gay Liberation Movement era when a community of her peers in sexual preference did not exist."[66]

Then in 1963 her fiery strength began to fail. She had fainting spells and attacks of nausea. Walking upstairs left her weak. On April 12, 1963, she wrote in her diary, "Tuesday had some weird attack. Almost conked out. Went to Dr. on Wednesday. Results: Sick girl. Hospital on the 20th. Enjoying the attention mightily."[67]

Her journal from May says, "I am writing this from a hospital bed; they have discovered that I have ulcers and anemia and here I am. Nothing serious but enough to keep me out of action for a bit."[68] What she doesn't say, what Robert Nemiroff believed she never knew, is that she had cancer.

Chapter

6 If You Were Dying Tomorrow, How Would You Live Today?

Lorraine and Robert never used the word "cancer" in discussing Lorraine's illness, nor did they admit to each other how sick she was. It was clear, however, that the illness was very serious. Throughout the remainder of her life, Lorraine would have to struggle to work.

In the summer of 1963 she had two operations that revealed cancer of the pancreas. In later years a treatment was developed for this disease, but in 1963 it was incurable. For a while after her surgery she recovered her strength and was able to work productively on *The Sign in Sidney Brustein's Window* and *Les Blancs* while doing research on the feminist Mary Wollstonecraft for another play. When *Brustein's Window* first came to life on paper, she wrote in her journal:

> The magic has come: about an hour ago! A torrent of what I have been trying to write all along. The people I know in the Village and not a stagey version of them. It will be all right now—a lot of work. But I know *what* I am writing now. It came all at once while I was in the kitchen and I wrote fourteen pages in an hour that will hardly need revision I think. Thank God, thank God! I could not have stood much more.[69]

By the fall of 1964 *Brustein* was finished and ready to go into production.

For some time, despite her marital problems, Hansberry had been unable to make a decision about a divorce. As long ago as 1957 she had described her conflict in a letter to the *Ladder*, an early lesbian publication:

> Isn't the problem of the married lesbian woman that of an individual who finds that, despite her conscious will oft times, she is inclined to have her most intense emotional and physical reactions directed toward other women, quite beyond any comparative thing she might have ever felt for her husband—whatever her sincere affection for him? And isn't that the problem? How one quite admits that to oneself—and to one's husband?[70]

Hansberry is described by feminist Adrienne Rich as a brilliant, ardent, and very angry woman whose life was limited by society's rules and expectations of her. Rich says:

> Fame and economic security are not enough to enable the woman artist—Black or white—to push her art and thought to their outermost limits. For that, we need community—a

community whose members know our experience from the inside out because it is their own, who will support us in our efforts to depict that experience in the face of those who would either reward us for glossing over, or punish us for articulating, the extremity in which we live.[71]

In the last months of her life, Hansberry may have felt that she needed to reduce the amount of energy expended on maintaining her image. Perhaps she wanted the support and understanding of a community such as Rich described. In any event, her primary emotional ties had been with her close women friends, with the result that the cost of remaining married had become too high for Lorraine. By March 1964 she and Robert had been living apart for several years, and at this time they were quietly divorced. They continued to work together, however, promoting civil rights and producing *Sidney Brustein*. The divorce remained a secret known only to their closest friends until the reading of her will in 1965.

Writing a Documentary

With a clearness about what was important to her, Lorraine began devoting her draining energy to her writing and work in the civil rights movement. In the same month

---

Longing to Be a Rebel

Hansberry's illness kept her from doing more for civil rights. Yet she did not feel that speeches, fundraising, and writing were enough; she longed to join the activists on the front lines. In this excerpt from her journal, which appears in To Be Young, Gifted and Black, *she writes:*

"Do I remain a revolutionary? Intellectually—without a doubt. But am I prepared to give my body to the struggle or even my *comforts*? This is what I puzzle about."

And later: "Have the feeling I should throw myself back into the movement. Become a human being again.

But that very impulse is immediately flushed with a thousand vacillations and forbidding images. I see myself lying in a pool of perspiration in a dark tenement room recalling Croton and the trees and longing for death—

Comfort has come to be its own corruption. I think of lying without a pain-killer in pain. In all the young years no such image ever occurred to me. I rather *looked forward* to going to jail once. Now I can hardly imagine surviving it at all. Comfort. Apparently I have sold my soul for it.

I think when I get my health back I shall go into the south to find out what kind of revolutionary I am."

---

that she ended her marriage, she began her last major civil rights project, a photo documentary for the Student Nonviolent Coordinating Committee, a group of young people interested in working for civil rights by organizing demonstrations and voter registration drives.

SNCC photographers were putting together a history of the fight for civil rights in the South, and Hansberry had agreed to write the text. During the project she became increasingly ill. She struggled against waves of pain and later contended with the sedation and confusion of painkillers while she leafed through photographs for the book. But she fought off illness to complete the project, which she believed portrayed the most important living drama of her time.

The book, published in 1964 and entitled *The Movement: Documentary of a Struggle for Equality*, begins with the picture of a two-lane paved road and Hansberry's text: "This is the road from Jackson to Yazoo City, leading into the Mississippi Delta country, the heart of the Deep South."[72] She placed familiar pictures of peaceful southern countryside next to photos of lynchings, poverty, and industry. She showed segregated water fountains, examples of what she called

> All the complicated silliness that a system took so much trouble to create. . . .
>
> The laws which enforce segregation do not presume the inferiority of a people; they assume an inherent equalness. It is the logic of the lawmakers that if a society does not erect artificial barriers between the people . . . the people might fraternize and give their attention to the genuine, shared problems of the community.[73]

Hansberry wrote captions to photos of lynchings, beatings, and Ku Klux Klan activities as well as marches, music making, and prayers. She commented on photos of police dogs and armed officers as follows:

> What the dogs and guns and hoses have proved is that the entire power structure of the South must be altered. The original demand for equal treatment on buses and at lunch counters has had to broaden and sharpen, to strike at the political base of Negro oppression . . . by demanding the vote. In doing so, the Negro has tried to gain the protection of the Federal Government. For the most part, it has been a futile effort.[74]

The book concludes with pictures of young revolutionaries and the words: "They stand in the hose fire at Birmingham; they stand in the rain at Hattiesburg. They are young, they are beautiful, they are determined. It is for us to create, now, an America that deserves them."[75]

"To Be Young, Gifted and Black"

In the spring and summer of the year she worked on *The Movement*, Lorraine was in and out of the hospital as the cancer was diagnosed and treated. In May, although she was receiving radiation and chemotherapy, her doctors agreed to release her for one day, to honor a commitment to speak to the winners of the United Negro College Fund writing contest. In her speech, "The Nation Needs Your Gifts," she introduced the now famous phrase "to be young, gifted and black." It was a passionate

Throughout her life, Lorraine Hansberry worked to better the lives of America's youth and to encourage them in their endeavors.

speech written to inspire the students and celebrate their accomplishment. Of the long history of black accomplishments in this country she said:

> . . . the American black man . . . first began publishing his newspapers in 1827 while the greatest of his number were still in chains. He began writing classical verse before America was a nation. . . . And that is why I say that, though it be a thrilling and marvelous thing to be merely young and gifted in such times, it is doubly so—doubly dynamic—to be young, gifted *and black.*

Look at the work that awaits you! There is a story to be told and retold again until no man can plead his ignorance.[76]

She urged the young people to use their writing talents to better the human race:

> Write if you will: but write about the world as it is and as you think it OUGHT to be and must be—if there is to be a world. Write about not only exotic disappointments—but ordinary ones. Write about the sit-ins; write about the lady who bored you on the

airplane; write about how the stars seem viewed from earth. . . . Write! Work hard at it, CARE about it. . . . And write about our people, tell their story.[77]

By Whatever Means Necessary

Hansberry continued to be ill and in bed for much of June, but despite her condition she agreed to public appearances she deemed important. For example, she participated in a debate billed as "Black Revolution and White Backlash," put on in New York by the Association of Artists for Freedom. Blacks on the panel such as Ossie Davis, Ruby Dee, Lorraine Hansberry, and LeRoi Jones defended the growing use of force by civil rights activists. The white liberals on the panel were supportive of the movement, but they predicted that many other whites would react to the increasing use of force by black civil rights activists with a rejecting "backlash." They criticized the use of force because they wanted changes to be accomplished peacefully and without violence.

During the discussion Lorraine defended blacks' taking drastic action. For example, she justified a traffic "stall-in" in which members of CORE stopped traffic on the Triboro Bridge connecting Manhattan with outlying parts of New York City. She believed that whites, not blacks,

Martin Luther King Jr. leads the March on Washington. Hansberry often grew impatient with the idea of peaceful protest, believing that blacks may have to repay violence with violence.

were the ones who needed to change their behavior. She explained that "we have to find some way . . . to encourage the white liberal to stop being a liberal and become an American radical."[78] She wanted whites as committed to equality as blacks, and as willing to risk their lives.

Hansberry defended a militant response to the bombing of black churches and to the lynching of blacks. She argued that generations of blacks had been working through peaceful, legal channels with little result. Their patience had been exhausted and it was not unreasonable to "lie down in the streets, tie up traffic, stop ambulances, do whatever we can, take to the hills if necessary with some guns and fight back."[79] This talk of force upset the panel moderator, white television journalist David Susskind, who argued that violence would only create more problems. To Susskind's call for "less heat and more rational thought," Hansberry responded:

> I'm a little surprised that you got quite as exercised as you did about some of the things that were said here. I know that you, for instance, are an admirer of our late President [John Kennedy] and he presumed . . . to have suggested to the world that if our foreign policy were not honored with regard to Cuba that we would blow up the world, you see. And we live in a nation where everything is talked about in terms of the fact that we are going to be the mightiest, the toughest cats going, you know, in the whole world. And when a Negro says something about I'm tired, I can't stand it no more, I want to hit somebody, you say that we're sitting here panting and ranting for violence, you know. It's not right.

> I think it's very simple. . . . [T]he whole idea of debating whether or not Negroes should defend themselves is an insult. If anybody comes and does ill in your home and your community, obviously you try your best to kill them.

Susskind reacted to Hansberry's comparison of black activists' use of force with the government's threat of force against Cuba as follows: "Your playwriting is superb, but your dialectics [reasoning by which a conclusion is reached] is somewhat wanting. I fail to see what President Kennedy's decision at the Cuba showdown had to do with the black-white dialogue."[80]

James Wechsler of the *New York Post* said later that what he most remembered of that passionate debate was "the wounded eyes of Lorraine Hansberry; it was she who tried hardest to speak to all of us, more in injury than in wrath, and with a fiery loveliness."[81]

Brustein Opens on Broadway

While receiving treatment for her cancer she continued work on *The Sign in Sidney Brustein's Window*. During this time she saw Nemiroff frequently. He remained supportive of Hansberry during her illness and, together with his friend Burt D'Lugoff, began to produce *The Sign in Sidney Brustein's Window*. Early in October 1964 rehearsals began, and Hansberry moved with her typewriter and a nurse from Croton-on-Hudson to the Hotel Victoria to be closer to the Longacre Theatre where her play was to be performed. This play had been easy to finance after the success of *A Raisin in the Sun*, but for Lor-

A poster advertises Hansberry's play The Sign in Sidney Brustein's Window. *The play did not do well, and Robert Nemiroff urged audiences to tell others of the play to keep it running for Lorraine, who was ill with cancer.*

raine, the opening on Broadway was difficult. Sitting near the back in a wheelchair, she was an almost skeletal figure, barely able to respond to the greetings of her friends when the play ended. Then she returned to the hotel to wait for the reviews.

The published reports were disappointing. Critics had expected to see another play about blacks, but *The Sign in Sidney Brustein's Window* is about Greenwich Village and the white artists and intellectuals who lived there in the 1960s. The characters' abstract, intellectual con-

versations also disappointed reviewers. One claimed that the play was "depressing, diffuse and confusing . . . too many stories . . . too much talk."[82]

Many in the audience, however, loved the play. It wasn't only the uplifting message—we must care about our world, we must reach out and touch one another—audiences also loved the humor, the characters who were heartbreakingly alive, and the absorbing story.

Keeping the Play Alive

But *Sidney Brustein* was not a big hit like *Raisin.* Sales did not go well, and it became a struggle to keep the play going. *A Raisin in the Sun* had played for nineteen months on Broadway, but it was feared that *The Sign in Sidney Brustein's Window* would not last a week. Each night the curtain went down on Sidney's closing lines, ". . . weep now, darling, weep. Let us both weep. That is the first thing: to let ourselves feel again. . . . Then, tomorrow, we shall make something strong of this sorrow."[83] Each night, Robert Nemiroff, as producer, got up in front of the audience and told of the efforts to keep the play alive.

Groups of supporters bought ads in the *New York Times* urging people to see the play. An alphabetical list of signers included writers, playwrights, directors, and performers, black and white: Alan Alda, Steve Allen, James Baldwin, Anne Bancroft, Marlon Brando, Mel Brooks, Paddy Chayefsky, Ossie Davis, Sammy Davis Jr., Ruby Dee, Arthur Godfrey, Julie Harris, Lillian Hellman, Mike Nichols, Robert Preston, Lloyd Richards, Diana Sands, and Shelley Winters.

Gabriel Dell stars in The Sign in Sidney Brustein's Window *at the Longacre Theatre.*

One afternoon performance was attended by fifty ministers and rabbis who, after the performance, met with the actors and talked about the impact of the play. James Baldwin joined the discussion. The son of a Baptist minister who at one time wanted to be a preacher himself, Baldwin left work on a movie to help support the play. He admitted to the group that at first he had disliked the play. His distaste had turned to mixed feelings and finally to admiration. He explained that Lorraine's second play caused him to look inside himself at his own motives and actions in a way no play had done for a very long time. "If it cannot survive," he said, "then we are in trouble . . . because it is about nothing less than our responsibility to ourselves and each other."[84]

By this time Lorraine was too ill to write. When she lost all feeling from her chest to her toes, the doctors knew the cancer had spread to her nervous system, and Lorraine was taken to the hospital for the last time. There was not much to be done for the ailing playwright, who became blind and fell into a coma. There were, however, small miracles ahead for the ailing play. Actors and producers, members of the audience, and shareholders believed in the play. They stepped forward and offered money to keep it alive.

Both the playwright and her play received a reprieve—for a time. Amazingly, Lorraine came out of her coma and gradually over several weeks was able to see, to sit up in a chair, to visit with her friends, and to hear of the efforts people were making for her last play.

A Special Performance

A group of writers, actors, and producers put together an invitation to a special Sunday matinee performance for the theatrical community. Usually there are no Sunday matinees on Broadway. It is the performers' day off. To support Lorraine's play the cast and crew of *Brustein* were willing to give up their Sunday to allow other crews to see her play. The invitations were tacked up on the backstage bulletin boards of the New York theaters:

The show must go on . . . *my* show, baby, not yours!

This is the selfish truth as we in show business too often have come to know it. But once in a blue moon, a phenomenon occurs. Actors, directors, producers, playwrights, gently lay aside their megalomania and join hands in a common cause. . . .

Last week we saw that play. We had joined the cause originally out of respect for Lorraine Hansberry, but on the way to the theatre we secretly figured it was a bomb. . . .

We were shocked.

It was a *wonderful* play.

We laughed, we cried, we *thought*. In our opinion . . . *Brustein* . . . is a more mature and compelling work than Miss Hansberry's award-winning *A Raisin in the Sun*.

If there is in you one single filament of curiosity that glows to know what is happening in our theatre today, see it! Now![85]

Actors convinced friends to see the play. They spoke in front of theater groups who bought big blocks of tickets. Ministers and rabbis preached about it. Each time a closing notice was printed for the play, hundreds of people joined together to keep it going.

While the play was never a financial success, Hansberry succeeded in doing what was most important to her. She created characters who touched people's lives and made them think. To her, every person was a possible hero, and each of her characters allowed her to "reach a little closer to the world . . . to people . . . to see if we can share some illuminations together about each other."[86]

Hansberry's depiction of Sidney Brustein has been called one of the most successful dramatic characterizations of a Jew. As the hero he is a sensitive and moral man, but he also belittles his wife and is cruel to gays and harsh to his racist sister-in-law. As the play progresses he overcomes his weakness and prejudice to understand the world and move to change things. One sister-in-law, Mavis, is as complex as Sidney.

Sidney as Hero

In his book Hansberry's Drama, *scholar Steven Carter writes about the character of Sidney Brustein, who confronts his own prejudices and weaknesses. He deals with a prejudice important to Lorraine: society's attitude toward women.*

"Sidney himself, despite his unusually large understanding of his culture and the nature of prejudice, displays certain types of bigotry, the most significant of which is his attitude toward women, especially his wife. Ironically, while remaining a sensitive Jewish liberal who cares deeply about the sufferings of others . . . Sidney compels his wife to distort her character by living up to his fantasy image of her. He pressures Iris into playing the role of a spritely, barefooted mountain girl in his fantasy of living Thoreau-like in the pure air of the mountains as part of his attempt to cope with the strain of residing in New York City. It seems clear, though, that no matter how sympathetic Sidney is . . . his actions are chauvinistic; what he does is highly damaging to his wife and his relationship with her. . . . Sidney's chauvinistic fantasies drive Iris away from him because she increasingly feels the need to live in accordance with her . . . inner realities and drives. Only at the play's end, when Sidney seems more able to face reality in general and the reality of women in particular, is Iris willing to return to him."

Gabriel Dell and Rita Moreno in a scene from Brustein.

Middle class and conservative, she is prejudiced against Jews and blacks. She also shows courage by enduring a faithless marriage and tries to rid herself of prejudice. Sidney's wife, Iris, though a tolerant person, is not compassionate. As the story unfolds she finds the strength to leave the marriage and Sidney's unrealistic fantasies about her. She courageously pursues her own dreams.

Nearing the End

For the last two months of her life Hansberry had her sight and some movement in her lower body. Although cancer had entered her brain, she continued to be alert, expressing her sense of humor until her last few days.

Realizing, finally, that she was dying, she made out a will. She set up a trust fund for writers and civil rights groups to continue the struggle for freedom. When, at last, Lorraine did not have the strength to write, she knew she was near death. Her last words, on a tape recorder, are the words of a spiritual: "My Lord calls me. He calls me by the thunder. I ain't got long to stay here."[87]

On January 12, 1965, Lorraine Hansberry died. That night, after 101 performances, *The Sign in Sidney Brustein's Window* closed on Broadway.

Chapter

7 The Funeral

As hundreds of Lorraine's friends and family members gathered for the funeral, a blizzard raged outside the Harlem church. Among the mourners were writers and theater people. Alice Childress was there; Malcolm X sat quietly in a pew.

Paul Robeson stood and spoke of the privilege of working with Lorraine on his paper *Freedom*. Saying he admired her feelings for her people and her knowledge of their history, he called her work a precious heritage and finished by quoting an old folk song:

> Sometimes I feel like a mourning dove
> Sometimes I feel like a mourning dove
> Feel like a mourning dove.

> Sometimes I feel like an eagle in the air
> Sometimes I feel like an eagle in the air
> Feel like an eagle in the air.

"As Lorraine says farewell, she bids us keep our heads high and to hold on to our strength and power; to soar like the eagle."[88]

Other speakers praised Hansberry's role in the civil rights struggle. A telegram from Dr. King was read, as well:

> Her commitment of spirit, . . . her creative literary ability and her profound grasp of the deep social issues confronting the world today will re-

Hansberry died of cancer on January 12, 1965. Her funeral was attended by many well-known people, including Malcolm X and Alice Childress.

main an inspiration to generations yet unborn.

If I may paraphrase the words of Shakespeare's *Romeo and Juliet*: "If she should die take her and cut her into little stars and she will make the face of heaven so fine that all the world will be in love with night."[89]

The funeral procession left the church and wound its way through the blizzard north to Croton-on-Hudson, where Hansberry was buried in Bethel Cemetery.

For her tombstone, shaped like an open book, Nemiroff selected parts of two separate speeches by Sidney Brustein:

> I care Wally. . . . It takes too much energy not to care. Yesterday I counted twenty-six gray hairs on the top of my head—all from trying not to care. . . . The why of why we are here is an intrigue for adolescents; the how is what must command the living. Which is why I have lately become—an insurgent again![90]

A Self-Portrait

Hansberry's thought and writing has influenced the generations who followed her. Only a small part of her work was known at her death, but as Hansberry's first literary executor, Robert Nemiroff gradually released edited versions of her unpublished work. He dug into the three filing cabinets in her study and used what was there to create a collage of her life. He published *To Be Young, Gifted and Black: An Informal Autobiography of Lorraine Hansberry*; it contains excerpts from her unfinished novel, *All the Dark and Beautiful Warriors*, and essays and memoirs, speeches, and portions of private journals. Condensing and combining her words, he selected what he felt was important to fashion a picture of the woman he had married. He said of it:

It is a self-portrait, in that the words, experiences, characters and creations—including all the artwork . . .—are the artist's own. But it is also an adaptation, a portrait rendered through the perspective of another's eyes. And therefore it takes a somewhat novel form: biography and autobiography, part fact, part fiction, an act of creation and re-creation.[91]

Although Nemiroff initially envisioned *To Be Young, Gifted and Black* as a play, he could find no one interested in producing it. Then WBAI, the Public Radio station in New York City, decided to air a program on the second anniversary of Hansberry's death. It became a giant project, three months in the producing, and seven and a half hours long. The public response was so positive that Nemiroff was encouraged. Discarding the idea of a play, he revised his materials into a book. In 1969 an adaptation of the book began a successful run off-Broadway at the Cherry Lane Theatre. The production was financed by Harry Belafonte. After Broadway *To Be Young, Gifted and Black* had a successful two-year national tour and a television production. After seeing the play, Lorraine's friend Nina Simone wrote the song "To Be Young, Gifted and Black," which became very popular. At New York's Philharmonic Hall, Simone introduced her song as follows:

> I want to talk about a friend . . . it seems that she comes alive more and more—there are all kinds of things written about her each day—and I'm talking about Lorraine Hansberry. Dig that. "To Be Young, Gifted and Black" is the story of her life and . . . each time I do it she comes a little bit closer and I miss her a little bit more.[92]

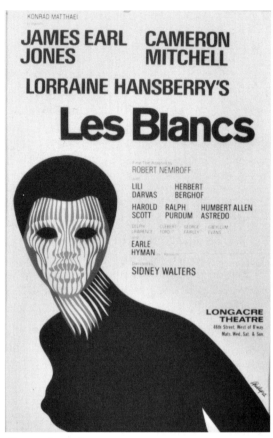

After Hansberry's death, Robert Nemiroff collected many of her works and prepared them for production. Here are posters from the productions of To Be Young, Gifted and Black and Les Blancs.

Eight years after Lorraine's death, Nemiroff wrote *Raisin*, a musical based on *A Raisin in the Sun* using unproduced material that Hansberry had written for early versions of the play. *Raisin* won the Tony Award in 1974 and, in 1975, a Grammy for best musical.

Les Blancs

Nemiroff also put the finishing touches on *Les Blancs*, completing unfinished scenes and tightening the drama with material from earlier drafts. As it went into production, many more people contributed to the project, helping to interpret and then produce it, trying to remain true to Lorraine's vision. *Les Blancs* was published in 1972 in *Lorraine Hansberry: The Collected Last Plays*, which also includes *The Drinking Gourd* and *What Use Are Flowers*.

Les Blancs opened at the Longacre Theatre on November 15, 1970. People responded strongly to the play, with audiences taking sides: some for the black man who became a revolutionary, some for the white liberals. Some thought the play encouraged black violence and revolution. Others sympathized with the struggle for liberation and cheered for the struggling African people. The critics were as divided as the audience and framed their discussions of the play to reflect their feelings about the central question. Hansberry was not trying to advocate revolution, however, but to use the theater to explore racism and spotlight the liberation struggles emerging around the world. She was asking in the play "Can there be revolution without violence?" She was not offering a final answer but hoping to open a dialogue. She wanted to show that actions have consequences, that one people cannot own another.

A Reputation for Activism

Hansberry captured the black experience and put it on stage truthfully. She worked as social activist. Feeling the oppression of being a woman, she used paper and pen both as her weapons and as her defense. She was a black woman who refused to stay in "her place." For these many

The musical Raisin *included material that Hansberry had originally written for her play but that had been cut when it was produced.*

achievements and for the literature she created and left behind, her reputation has continued to grow.

For a time after her death Hansberry's work was not valued, her name almost forgotten. Hansberry's work seemed too mild for the emerging black radicals. According to the principles of the new Black Arts drama of these radicals, strong female characters sabotaged the black image and crippled the black male. Hansberry, who wrote of strong women, whose male char-

---

Keeping Hansberry's Work Alive

Robert Nemiroff's play and book To Be Young, Gifted and Black *kept Hansberry's work before the public. At his death he was working on publishing* A Raisin in the Sun: The Unfilmed Screenplay. *In a foreword to the book, his widow, Jewell Gresham Nemiroff, credited Nemiroff for keeping Hansberry's work alive.*

"Hansberry's greatest gift to Bob was that, through her creativity, she gave him access to the magic of theater that had been since his graduate work in literary criticism and theater at New York University his deepest love. For him, the theater was forever exciting and rewarding. . . .

His greatest gift to Hansberry was his faith in the dramatic and literary outpourings of this woman who had declared to him with certainty: 'I am a writer. I am going to write!' and his sustained commitment, with the writer prematurely gone, to make certain that what she wrote would live."

Because of Hansberry's untimely death, much of her work remained unfinished. Her former husband and longtime friend Robert Nemiroff tried to rework and revise these unfinished works.

For a while after Hansberry's death, A Raisin in the Sun *fell out of favor with blacks, who saw racism in the characters of Walter Lee and Lena.*

acters were complete with strengths and weaknesses, who created white characters as well as black, was shunted aside. It took the next generation of blacks and feminists, twenty-five years later, to come to appreciate Hansberry and her art.

With the growth of women's theater and feminist criticism, Hansberry has been discovered by a new generation. A modern reading of her plays shows her as a true feminist. Her portrayals of women characters and the problems they took on challenged stereotypes and brought femi-

nist issues to the stage. Biographer Margaret Wilkerson writes:

Recently uncovered documents revealing Hansberry's sensitivity to homophobic attitudes have further stimulated feminist interest in her work. When more of her papers are released for publication, the full scope of Lorraine Hansberry's work will be appreciated and assessed.[93]

Hansberry's papers are under the control of her present literary executor, Jewell

The Dark Vision of Lorraine Hansberry

Hansberry biographer Margaret Wilkerson wrote of the playwright's vision becoming less hopeful. The endings of her plays are filled with pain and questions. In "The Dark Vision of Lorraine Hansberry," Wilkerson speculates about what would have happened if Lorraine had not died so young.

"When reflecting on Hansberry's death, one cannot help but wonder how she would have fared in the Broadway theater of subsequent years, had she lived. Would she have been 'the black darling' of the American theater? Would her later works have been received as enthusiastically as *A Raisin in the Sun*? The reception of her later plays suggests that the outpouring of praise for *A Raisin in the Sun* would not have ensured her continued success in the theater. . . . Had she lived, would her voice have received an audience on the main stage? Or would her work, like that of so many black writers, have been excluded from major commercial theaters? One would like to believe that Hansberry's sensibility and superior craftsmanship would protect her. But the history of American theater argues otherwise. . . .

Hansberry's vision was indeed 'dark'—colored by her experience and second sight as a fiercely independent black woman. This darkness pervaded her personal life as well—as loneliness, fear of her own debasement and despair of humankind always threatened to overwhelm her. Like Sidney and so many of her other characters, by sheer force of will she imposed a reason for life on life, despite all evidence to the contrary."

Gresham Nemiroff, who married Robert Nemiroff in 1967 and took over Hansberry's papers in 1991, upon Nemiroff's death. Because the papers are not available in a library or archive, further study and interpretation has been limited. In an essay, "The Problem of Lorraine Hansberry," feminist lesbian critic Adrienne Rich writes:

Lorraine Hansberry is a problem to me because she is Black, female and dead. Her work and her biography have come to us largely through the efforts of her literary executor and divorced husband Robert Nemiroff, who put together . . . the work which, though it is a collage of her words, is a pattern of his construction.

Biography [*To Be Young, Gifted and Black*] it may be. . . . But biography by a former husband and literary executor is not the same as autobiography. . . .

Yet this is the major lens through which Hansberry's life has been viewed. And it is frustrating to me that the Hansberry papers are not simply accessible in an archive open to the public; that students of Black and female history and literature, students of theater, cannot examine freely and draw conclusions about the mass of material from which *To Be Young, Gifted and Black* was sifted and selected. . . .

Lorraine Hansberry remains a problem and a challenge. I wait for the Black feminist who, with free access to Hansberry's unpublished papers, can help us see her unidealized, unsimplified, in her fullest complexity, in her fullest political context.[94]

What is readily known about Hansberry's life is that it is an example of the power of mixing art and politics. Besides being in the forefront of the civil rights movement, she fought oppression in all its guises. In addition to her well-known association with Paul Robeson when he was being hounded by McCarthy, and her work for SNCC and other primarily black groups, she challenged sexist attitudes and championed civil rights for homosexuals.

Two of Hansberry's plays were produced during her short career as a playwright, and these form a major contribution to American theater. *A Raisin in the Sun* was more than simply a "first" to be recorded in history books and never seen again. It opened doors for a generation of black artists in the theater and has become an American classic.

A Universal Playwright

Hansberry is one of the nation's best black playwrights and a major American dramatist. She wrote five compelling plays that cover many continents and cultures. Her range of subjects is imposing. Hansberry scholar Steven Carter states that Hansberry "was among the most universal playwrights of her time. Few others . . . even attempted to write dramas about as many different cultures and periods."[95]

In 1979 *Freedomways* devoted an entire issue to a tribute. In "Lorraine Hansberry: Art of Thunder, Vision of Light," editor Jean Carey Bond wrote that Hansberry's skill ranked her with the best modern American writers.

> She was a particular American—a black female American writer who grew up in a comfortable home on the South Side of Chicago. But in her singularity . . . she was a voice of the whole United States, of its dynamic culture and its tortured politics. . . . Lorraine embraced the United States . . . not only the life she found on Chicago's South Side, but the difficult, painful history which had placed her there.[96]

Notes

Introduction: A Woman Ahead of Her Time

1. Woodie King Jr., "Lorraine Hansberry's Children: Black Artists and *A Raisin in the Sun*," in Jean Carey Bond, ed., *Freedomways: A Quarterly Review of the Freedom Movement*, vol. 19, no. 4, 1979, p. 220.

2. Lorraine Hansberry, adapted by Robert Nemiroff, *To Be Young, Gifted and Black: An Informal Autobiography of Lorraine Hansberry*. New York: Penguin Books, 1970, p. 222.

3. Quoted in Steven R. Carter, *Hansberry's Drama*. New York: Penguin Books, 1993, pp. 11–12.

Chapter 1: An Insurgent

4. Lorraine Hansberry, "The Negro Writer and His Roots: Toward a New Romanticism," *Black Scholar*, March/April 1981, p. 11.

5. Hansberry, *To Be Young, Gifted and Black*, pp. 48–49.

6. Lorraine Hansberry, "All the Dark and Beautiful Warriors," excerpted in *Village Voice*, August 16, 1983, p. 11.

7. Hansberry, *To Be Young, Gifted and Black*, p. 50.

8. Hansberry, *To Be Young, Gifted and Black*, p. 48.

9. Hansberry, *To Be Young, Gifted and Black*, p. 53.

10. Lorraine Hansberry, "The Scars of the Ghetto," *Monthly Review*, vol. 41, no. 3, February 1965, p. 53.

11. Quoted in Harold R. Isaacs, *The New World of Negro Americans*. New York: John Day, 1963, p. 285.

12. Quoted in Isaacs, *The New World of Negro Americans*, p. 284.

Chapter 2: An Education of Many Kinds

13. Anne Cheney, Preface to *Lorraine Hansberry*. Boston: Twayne Publishers, 1984.

14. Lorraine Hansberry, "Playwrighting: Creative Constructiveness," *Annals of Psychotherapy*, vol. 5, no. 1, 1964, pp. 13–17.

15. Quoted in Arnold Rampersad, *The Life of Langston Hughes, Vol. II, 1941–1967, I Dream a World*. New York: Oxford University Press, 1988, pp. 297–98.

16. Hansberry, *To Be Young, Gifted and Black*, p. 51.

17. Quoted in "Talk of the Town," *New Yorker*, May 5, 1959, p. 34.

18. Cheney, *Lorraine Hansberry*, p. 67.

19. Hansberry, *To Be Young, Gifted and Black*, p. 74.

20. Quoted in "Talk of the Town," *New Yorker*, pp. 33–35.

21. Hansberry, *To Be Young, Gifted and Black*, p. 87.

22. Hansberry, *To Be Young, Gifted and Black*, pp. 90–91.

23. Hansberry, *To Be Young, Gifted and Black*, p. 93.

Chapter 3: New York! New York!

24. Michael G. Kort, *The Cold War*. Brookfield, CT: Millbrook Press, 1994, p. 66.

25. Hansberry, *To Be Young, Gifted and Black*, pp. 97–98.

26. Cheney, *Lorraine Hansberry*, pp. 47, 53.

27. Quoted in Cheney, *Lorraine Hansberry*, p. 47.

28. Hansberry, *To Be Young, Gifted and Black*, pp. 102–103.

29. Carter, *Hansberry's Drama*, p. 5.

30. Lorraine Hansberry, "Life Challenges Negro Youth," *Freedom*, March 1955, p. 7.

31. Margaret B. Wilkerson, "The Dark Vision of Lorraine Hansberry: Excerpts from a Literary Biography," *Massachusetts Review*, vol. 28, no. 4, Winter 1987, pp. 645ff.

32. Cheney, *Lorraine Hansberry*, p. 43.

33. Lorraine Hansberry, *Les Blancs: The Collected Last Plays*, Robert Nemiroff, ed. New York: Random House/Vintage Books, 1994, p. xvi.

34. Quoted in "Talk of the Town," *New Yorker*, p. 34.

35. Quoted in Carter, *Hansberry's Drama*, p. 135.

36. Quoted in Cheney, *Lorraine Hansberry*, p. 20.

37. Quoted in Margaret Wilkerson, "Lorraine Vivian Hansberry," in *Black Women in America: A Historical Encyclopedia*, Darlene Clark Hine, ed., vol. 1. Brooklyn, NY: Carlson Publishing, 1993, p. 527.

38. Lorraine Hansberry, "In Defense of the Equality of Men," in *The Norton Anthology of Literature by Women: The Tradition in English*, Sandra M. Gilbert and Susan Gubar, eds. New York: W. W. Norton, 1985, p. 2,064.

39. Hansberry, *To Be Young, Gifted and Black*, p. 105.

Chapter 4: Devoting Herself to Her Work

40. Lorraine Hansberry, *Lorraine Hansberry's A Raisin in the Sun/The Sign in Sidney Brustein's Window*. New York: New American Library, 1966, pp. 22–23.

41. Sharon Friedman, "Feminism as Theme in Twentieth-Century American Women's Drama," *American Studies*, vol. 25, no. 1, Spring 1984, p. 85.

42. Hansberry, "Playwrighting: Creative Constructiveness," p. 14.

43. Hansberry, *To Be Young, Gifted and Black*, p. 107.

44. Hansberry, "The Negro Writer and His Roots," p. 12.

45. Hansberry, "The Negro Writer and His Roots," p. 5.

46. Hansberry, "The Negro Writer and His Roots," p. 11.

47. Hansberry, *To Be Young, Gifted and Black*, pp. 108–109.

48. Lerone Bennett Jr. and Margaret G. Burroughs, "A Lorraine Hansberry Rap," in Bond, *Freedomways*, vol. 19, no. 4, 1979, p. 229.

49. Amiri Baraka, "A Critical Reevaluation: *A Raisin in the Sun*'s Enduring Passion," in *A Raisin in the Sun (Expanded Twenty-Fifth Anniversary Edition) and The Sign in Sidney Brustein's Window*, Robert Nemiroff, ed. New York: New American Library, 1987, pp. 19–20.

50. Margaret Wilkerson, ed., *Nine Plays by Black Women*. New York: New American Library, 1986, p. xx.

51. David Littlejohn, *Black on White: A Critical Survey of Writings by American Ne-*

groes. New York: Grossman Publishers, 1966, p. 65.

Chapter 5: Misunderstandings

52. Quoted in Ernest Kaiser and Robert Nemiroff, "A Lorraine Hansberry Bibliography," in Bond, *Freedomways*, p. 286.

53. Lorraine Hansberry, "The Nation Needs Your Gifts," *Negro Digest*, August 1964, p. 29.

54. Quoted in Studs Terkel, "Make New Sounds," *American Theatre*, November 1984, p. 5.

55. Steven R. Carter, "The John Brown Theatre: Lorraine Hansberry's Cultural Views and Dramatic Goals," in Bond, *Freedomways*, p. 190.

56. Lorraine Hansberry, *A Raisin in the Sun: The Unfilmed Original Screenplay.* New York: Penguin Books, 1994, p. 155.

57. Quoted in Hansberry, *Les Blancs*, p. 147.

58. Hansberry, *Les Blancs*, pp. 147–48.

59. Quoted in Hansberry, *Les Blancs*, p. 146.

60. Hansberry, *Les Blancs*, p. 122.

61. Hansberry, *To Be Young, Gifted and Black*, p. 168.

62. Hansberry, *To Be Young, Gifted and Black*, pp. 177, 181.

63. James Baldwin, "Lorraine Hansberry at the Summit," in Bond, *Freedomways*, p. 271.

64. Hansberry, *To Be Young, Gifted and Black*, p. 229.

65. Quoted in Carter, *Hansberry's Drama*, p. 6.

66. Carter, *Hansberry's Drama*, p. 5.

67. Hansberry, *To Be Young, Gifted and Black*, p. 226.

68. Hansberry, *To Be Young, Gifted and Black*, p. 227.

Chapter 6: If You Were Dying Tomorrow, How Would You Live Today?

69. Hansberry, *To Be Young, Gifted and Black*, p. 197.

70. Letter signed L. N., *Ladder*, vol. 1, no. 11, 1957, p. 27.

71. Adrienne Rich, *Blood, Bread and Poetry: Selected Prose 1979–1985.* New York: W. W. Norton, 1986, p. 22.

72. Lorraine Hansberry, *The Movement: Documentary of a Struggle for Equality.* New York: Simon & Schuster, 1964, p. 6.

73. Hansberry, *The Movement*, pp. 24–26.

74. Hansberry, *The Movement*, pp. 60–62.

75. Hansberry, *The Movement*, p. 122.

76. Hansberry, "The Nation Needs Your Gifts," p. 28.

77. Hansberry, "The Nation Needs Your Gifts," p. 29.

78. Transcript of panel discussion, "Black Revolution and White Blacklash," *National Guardian*, July 4, 1964, pp. 6–7.

79. "Black Revolution and White Backlash," pp. 5–9.

80. "Black Revolution and White Backlash," p. 8.

81. Robert Nemiroff, "From These Roots: Lorraine Hansberry and the South," *Southern Exposure*, September/October 1984, p. 35.

82. Quoted in Lorraine Hansberry, *Lorraine Hansberry's A Raisin in the Sun/The Sign in Sidney Brustein's Window.* New York: New American Library, 1966, p. 151.

83. Hansberry, *Lorraine Hansberry's A Raisin in the Sun/The Sign in Sidney Brustein's Window*, p. 318.

84. Quoted in Hansberry, *Lorraine Hansberry's A Raisin in the Sun/The Sign in Sidney Brustein's Window*, p. 164.

85. Quoted in Hansberry, *Lorraine Hansberry's A Raisin in the Sun/The Sign in Sidney Brustein's Window*, p. 168.

86. Hansberry, *To Be Young, Gifted and Black*, p. 34.

87. Quoted in Baldwin, "Lorraine Hansberry at the Summit," p. 272.

Chapter 7: The Funeral

88. Paul Robeson, in Bond, *Freedomways*, p. 222.

89. Martin Luther King Jr., in Bond, *Freedomways*, p. 212.

90. Quoted in Lonnie Elder III, "Lorraine Hansberry: Social Consciousness and the Will," in Bond, *Freedomways*, p. 218.

91. Quoted in Hansberry, *To Be Young, Gifted and Black*, p. xxii.

92. Quoted in Hansberry, *To Be Young, Gifted and Black*, p. 270.

93. Wilkerson, "Lorraine Vivian Hansberry," p. 528.

94. Rich, *Blood, Bread and Poetry*, pp. 12–13.

95. Carter, *Hansberry's Drama*, p. 15.

96. Jean Carey Bond, "Lorraine Hansberry: To Reclaim Her Legacy," in *Freedomways*, pp. 183–85.

For Further Reading

Books About Hansberry

Langston Hughes and Milton Meltzer, eds., *Black Magic: A Pictorial History of Black Entertainers in America*. New York: Bonanza Books, 1967. Interesting book full of pictures traces black entertainers beginning with the early minstrel shows. Two chapters, "A Raisin in the Sun" and "Negro Playwrights," which pictures Hansberry's friends and peers, are especially relevant.

Elizabeth C. Phillips, *The Works of Lorraine Hansberry: A Critical Commentary*. New York: Monarch Press, 1973. From the Monarch Notes literature series, this book includes a section of critical analysis, an overview of Hansberry's themes and style, reviews, and articles in addition to biographical information.

Catherine Scheader, *They Found a Way: Lorraine Hansberry*. Chicago: Campus Publications, 1978. A biography for young readers that contains original artwork by Hansberry and many family photographs.

Books About Hansberry's Time

Michael G. Kort, *The Cold War*. Brookfield, CT: Millbrook Press, 1994. Interesting and accessible history of the cold war including an assessment of the problems and possibilities left at the end of this long period in modern history.

Robin McKown, *The Colonial Conquest of Africa*. New York: Franklin Watts, 1971. A history of the scramble to colonize Africa illustrated with prints, photographs, and maps. Although well researched and readable, the book ends many years before the abolition of apartheid in South Africa.

Arnold Rampersad, *The Life of Langston Hughes, Vol. II, 1941–1967, I Dream a World*. New York: Oxford University Press, 1988. Definitive biography of poet who had major impact on Hansberry's life.

Documentary

Ralph J. Tangney, writer and producer, *Lorraine Hansberry: The Black Experience in the Creation of Drama*. Princeton, NJ: Films for the Humanities, 1976. Film of Hansberry's life and artistic growth largely in her own words and voice. Included are excerpts from the major plays.

Works by Hansberry

Les Blancs: The Collected Last Plays. Robert Nemiroff, ed. New York: Random House/Vintage Books, 1994. Besides *Les Blancs*, the play of African revolution, this book contains *The Drinking Gourd*, Hansberry's unproduced television play on slavery and the Civil War, and *What Use Are Flowers*, her pacifist television drama of survival after nuclear holocaust.

Lorraine Hansberry's A Raisin in the Sun/The Sign in Sidney Brustein's Window. New York: New American Library, 1966. This single-volume edition of Hansberry's two best-known plays also contains

Robert Nemiroff's essay "The 101 Final Performances of Sidney Brustein" with twelve pages of photographs. An American Playhouse television production of *A Raisin in the Sun* is available at many video stores.

The Movement: Documentary of a Struggle for Equality. New York: Simon & Schuster, 1964. Hansberry's stirring text for a collection of photos showing the historic battles for civil rights in the 1950s and early 1960s.

A Raisin in the Sun: The Unfilmed Original Screenplay. New York: Penguin Books, 1994. The unedited script for the movie Hansberry wanted to film.

Includes a foreword by her literary executor, a commentary by Spike Lee, and an introduction by Margaret Wilkerson of the University of California at Berkeley.

To Be Young, Gifted and Black: An Informal Autobiography of Lorraine Hansberry. Adapted by Robert Nemiroff. New York: Penguin Books, 1970. A collage of Hansberry's written words, private and public, edited by her literary executor, Robert Nemiroff, to whom she was married between 1953 and 1964. The material was later adapted into a successful play. The book includes original drawings and art.

Additional Works Consulted

Amiri Baraka, "A Critical Reevaluation: *A Raisin in the Sun*'s Enduring Passion," in *A Raisin in the Sun (Expanded Twenty-Fifth Anniversary Edition) and The Sign in Sidney Brustein's Window*, Robert Nemiroff, ed. New York: New American Library, 1987. Important lines and scenes cut in the original production are here restored. In this retrospective essay Baraka no longer considers it a conservative play. He views it as a statement of the African-American majority.

"Black Revolution and White Backlash," *National Guardian*, July 4, 1964. A panel discussion of black militants and white liberals arguing the growing use of confrontation in the civil rights movement.

Jean Carey Bond, ed., *Freedomways: A Quarterly Review of the Freedom Movement*, vol. 19, no. 4, 1979. This issue of the journal, entitled "Lorraine Hansberry: Art of Thunder, Vision of Light," is a tribute to the playwright with essays by the editor, James Baldwin, Lerone Bennett Jr. and Margaret Burroughs, Steven Carter, Lonnie Elder III, Alex Haley, Ernest Kaiser and Robert Nemiroff, Martin Luther King Jr., Woodie King Jr., Aishah Rahman, Adrienne Rich, Paul Robeson, and Margaret Wilkerson. Includes the most extensive Hansberry bibliography presently available.

Steven Carter, *Hansberry's Drama*. New York: Penguin Books, 1993. A well-written and thoughtful exploration of the subject's life with an emphasis on her drama. The chronology is especially thorough.

Anne Cheney, *Lorraine Hansberry*. Boston: Twayne Publishers, 1984. The most complete biography to date, it has some excessive, if interesting, digressions on notable figures in Hansberry's formative life: W. E. B. Du Bois, Paul Robeson, and Langston Hughes. Though very readable, it lacks analysis and does not explore Hansberry's feminism.

John Henrick Clarke, ed., et al, *Black Titan: W. E. B. Du Bois*. Boston: Beacon Press, 1970. An anthology by the editors of *Freedomways*. A compilation of articles by authors and public personalities about the importance of Du Bois and his work.

Sharon Friedman, "Feminism as Theme in Twentieth-Century American Women's Drama," *American Studies*, vol. 25, no. 4, Spring 1984. The plays of Hansberry, Susan Glaspell, Rachel Crothers, and Lillian Hellman. Interesting exploration of the evolution of feminine consciousness and social issues shown in American theater.

Sandra M. Gilbert and Susan Gubar, eds., *The Norton Anthology of Literature by Women: The Tradition in English*. New York: W. W. Norton, 1985. A comprehensive historical overview of the female literary tradition. Each author is introduced with biographical and critical notes. Hansberry's essay, "In Defense of the Equality of Men," protests what she viewed as absurd assumptions about race and sex. She is shown as a link between nineteenth-century abolitionist Sojourner Truth and contemporary black dramatists like Ntozake Shange.

Lorraine Hansberry, "All the Dark and Beautiful Warriors," excerpted in *Village Voice*, August 16, 1983. The unpublished, uncompleted novel.

Lorraine Hansberry, 1957 letter signed L. N. to the *Ladder*, 1.11:27, a periodical of the lesbian organization Daughters of Bilitis.

Lorraine Hansberry, "The Nation Needs Your Gifts," *Negro Digest*, August 1964. Text of a speech delivered to winners of a creative writing contest cosponsored by the *Reader's Digest* and the United Negro College Fund.

Lorraine Hansberry, "The Negro Writer and His Roots: Toward a New Romanticism," *Black Scholar*, March/April 1981. A speech to a major black writers conference in which she presented her credo, the challenge before black writers.

Lorraine Hansberry, "Playwrighting: Creative Constructiveness," a speech for a conference of psychotherapists which was published in *Annals of Psychotherapy*, vol. 5, no. 1, 1964. Celebrating black matriarchs.

Lorraine Hansberry, "The Scars of the Ghetto." This speech on the impact of Jim Crow laws given at a celebration for funding the purchase of *Monthly Review* press books for black college libraries. It was printed a month after her death in *Monthly Review*, February 1965.

Darlene Clark Hine, ed., *Black Women in America: An Historical Encyclopedia*, vol. 1. Brooklyn, NY: Carlson Publishing, 1993. The essay "Hansberry, Lorraine Vivian (1930–1965)" is perhaps a preview of the long-awaited biography by Margaret Wilkerson, professor of theater in the African American Studies Department at the University of California at Berkeley. Wilkerson has access to all of Hansberry's papers and has been working on a definitive biography since 1982. Her biography, *The Dark Side of Lorraine Hansberry*, will be published by Little, Brown.

Langston Hughes, *Selected Poems of Langston Hughes*. New York: Vintage Books, Random House, Inc., 1990. The poems in this collection were chosen by Hughes shortly before his death in 1967 and represent his entire career. It includes poems never before printed.

Harold R. Isaacs, *The New World of Negro Americans*. New York: John Day, 1963. An interesting exploration of how history affected African Americans through the early 1960s. This study by a journalist and international correspondent is based on interviews in which African Americans reveal their conceptions of themselves and society. The Hansberry interview is especially lively.

David Littlejohn, *Black on White: A Critical Survey of Writings by American Negroes*. New York: Grossman Publishers, 1966. A historical overview of writing by African Americans from before the Harlem Renaissance to the 1960s.

Robert Nemiroff, "From These Roots: Lorraine Hansberry and the South," an interesting essay exploring Hansberry's close connections to the South. Printed in *Southern Exposure*, vol. 12, September/October 1984.

Adrienne Rich, *Blood, Bread and Poetry: Selected Prose 1979–1985*. New York: W. W. Norton, 1986. Challenging essays of radical feminist. Questions the silencing of Hansberry as a feminist and lesbian.

"Talk of the Town," interview by columnist E. B. White for *New Yorker*, May 5, 1959. Interesting biographical material given in the flush of her first major success.

Studs Terkel, "Make New Sounds," an interview by the Chicago journalist and social commentator for his radio show "Almanac." Published in *American Theatre*, November 1984, at the twenty-fifth anniversary of the play's opening, this sensitive interview deals with many important issues in Hansberry's life and brings her strong personality alive.

Margaret Wilkerson, "The Dark Vision of Lorraine Hansberry: Excerpts from a Literary Biography." Essay, published in the *Massachusetts Review*, vol. 28, no. 4, Winter 1987, exploring her contradictions and increasingly pessimistic vision.

Margaret Wilkerson, ed., *Nine Plays by Black Women*. New York: New American Library, 1986. This anthology of plays from the 1950s will illumine any discussion of race, class, and gender. Contains an excerpt of Hansberry's favorite project, the never-completed opera *Toussaint*.

Index

Credits

About the Author

After thirty years as a health care professional, Janet Tripp earned a B.A. in English at the University of Minnesota. She has been an editor for *Hurricane Alice*, a feminist quarterly and has been published in several anthologies: *Between the Heartbeats: Poetry and Prose by Nurses* and two editions of *The Book Group Book.*

Ms. Tripp is a psychiatric nurse at Hennepin County Medical Center in Minneapolis, Minnesota, where she lives with her husband, Richard, and greyhound, Goldie.